SUBVERSIVE
CHRISTIANITY

SUBVERSIVE CHRISTIANITY

Imaging God
in a Dangerous Time

SECOND EDITION

Brian Walsh

WIPF & STOCK · Eugene, Oregon

Wipf and Stock Publishers
199 W 8th Ave, Suite 3
Eugene, OR 97401

Subversive Christianity, Second Edition
Imaging God in a Dangerous Time
By Walsh, Brian J.
Copyright©2014 by Walsh, Brian J.
ISBN 13: 978-1-4982-0340-1
Publication date 9/1/2014
Previously published by Alta Vista Press, 1992.

Contents

*For J Richard Middleton,
colleague, friend and teacher.*

Foreword

Where is Western culture going? And what should Christians think about it? Those who already ask these questions often come up with confused answers. Those who do not are, arguably, living in a fool's paradise (or possibly a fool's hell).

Brian Walsh tackles the central issues head on in this powerful little book. He is well equipped to do so. On the one hand he has studied contemporary culture, and a wide range of Christian discussions of it, in great depth. We are here given, in easily accessible form, the fruits of many years of patient academic work. On the other hand, he has drunk deeply from biblical theology, not least (as becomes clear) from the Old Testament, and provides clear and creative exegesis of several passages, and of one book in particular (Jeremiah) in a way which breathes new life into them. Several times, reading his exegesis, I found myself wanting to go off and preach on the passage in question. Walsh brings together the Bible and the modern world in a way which is as original as it is compelling.

Many books which offer a Christian response to the contemporary world fall into the trap of cheap denunciation, gloating over the failure of a particular political system. This book, conspicuously, does not. The critique of modern liberal democracy is mounted at the level of a serious argument, for instance in the illuminating discussion of Francis Fukuyama in Chapter 3. But the tone of voice is not that of the inverted triumphalist. It is our own culture that is dying on its feet: with Jeremiah, the appropriate response is tears. And, following Jeremiah's lead, the author sketches out not only the bad news but also the good. There is hope beyond what seems to some observers like 'the end of history'. We still have vital tasks to perform, as Christians and as human beings; and these tasks are to be informed not merely by polemic against contemporary evils but by hope in the God who, having created a beautiful world, is now intent on recreating it.

Brian Walsh is already well known to audiences in North America as a speaker and writer who has a lot of Christian wisdom to impart to our generation. This book will enhance that reputation, and extend it to British audiences as well. He is a scholar who knows how to communicate to a wide audience. He is a sensitive Christian who allows his head and his heart to work closely together in scholarship and life. And, as readers of this book will quickly discover, he is a lively and engaging writer. I am delighted to commend *Subversive Christianity*, and hope and believe that it will be effective in encouraging many Christians to explore the full implications of the extraordinary and radical message of the Gospel.

N T Wright
Worcester College, Oxford. May 1991

Preface

Some readers of this little book will at an earlier time have read my co-authored book, *The Transforming Vision: Shaping a Christian World View*. That book, written with J Richard Middleton, was first published in 1984 and has enjoyed a reception and influence that has gone far beyond its authors' first expectations.

A story concerning the completion of *The Transforming Vision* helps introduce *Subversive Christianity*. Richard and I were together in Montreal in December of 1983 and had just completed the final draft of the book. After writing the preface we realised, with joy and relief, that it was now really finished. We offered to God our prayers of thanksgiving, asked his blessing on our literary contribution to his kingdom and embraced each other. Richard then looked at me and said, 'You know, there is something that we have missed in this book.' After first thinking this to be an odd thing to say at this point, I began wondering what we had missed. Not enough on feminism, the environmental crisis, the nuclear threat? Of course more could have been said about any of these topics. But then Richard told me what he had on his mind. 'Nowhere in this book do we talk about suffering.' That was true, but why should that be an issue? Richard's answer was simple. Suffering is a central theme in Scripture, yet it was apparently absent from our depiction of a biblical worldview.

This book is not about suffering. In that sense it doesn't attempt to make up for what is lacking in *The Transforming Vision*. But this story does serve to introduce this book. The way in which I attempt to experience, live out and articulate a Christian worldview in my life, and here in this book, is now tempered by the experience of suffering in a way that was simply not possible in that earlier work. Themes and motifs that you will encounter throughout this book, such as captivity, exile, mourning, grief, pathos and weeping, have all been formed through the experience of suffering in my life. That personal suffering has also afforded me the opportunity to come to a deeper understanding of the suffering of other people, the rest of creation and even Christ's suffering on the cross. I have come to realise more fully that any worldview, if it is to be both biblical and illuminative of what human life is really like, must be a worldview that comprehends our brokenness and suffering. Biblically, there is no resurrection without a cross. Moreover, resurrection life is still a matter of bearing a cross, a 'filling up of what is lacking' in Christ's affliction (Col 1:24). It is in the context of such a spirituality that this book is written.

There are two people who have had the most profound influence on what I have written here. The first is none other than the person who knew so well what was missing in *The Transforming Vision*, Richard Middleton. It was almost as if Richard's comment was a prophecy for both of us. And I consider myself very fortunate to have had such a wise friend over the years. Richard's breadth of insight and depth of spirituality have been a constant source of strength and encouragement to me. I am aware of his influence throughout this book and gratefully dedicate it to him.

It was also Richard who introduced me to the writings of Old Testament scholar, Walter Brueggemann. He is the second person whose influence can be detected throughout this book. Brueggemann's creative and provocative scholarship has opened up new resources of biblical reflection for me. To him I acknowledge my debt.

The chapters of this book were first presented as addresses to receptive audiences throughout Canada, the United States and Britain. Without the encouragement of those audiences this book would not have been written. It was, however, the encouragement of British audiences, and more specifically the support of my student Paul Tuvey, and Steve Bishop from The Regius Press in Bristol that led to the bringing together of these addresses into one book.

To identify the audiences and contexts of each of these chapters would take too much space for a preface. However, I do think that it is important to say something about Chapter 3. That chapter, 'Waiting for a miracle: Christian grief at the end of history', was first presented as the Brock University Christianity and Culture lecture of 1990. The night of my lecture marked the second anniversary of the tragic death of my friend and co-worker, Michael Hare. Michael worked for Inter Varsity Christian Fellowship at Brock in St. Catherines, Ontario while I served as the Christian Reformed chaplain at the same university. His death in a car accident left behind his wife Catherine and their infant son. Leading a memorial service on campus and ministering to students who were close to Michael, as well as dealing with my own grief, is part of the suffering that I spoke about earlier. When Chapter 3 was presented at Brock University, I dedicated that address to Michael's memory. I want to honour that memory in this book as well.

Most fundamentally, this book is about worldview formation, and the worldview I am attempting to form is aptly described as a 'subversive Christianity'. Of course, that doesn't encompass all that I believe to be the case about Christian faith, but in a context of cultural captivity, combined with cultural collapse, one of the things that Christian faith must be is subversive. The only other option, as far as I can see, is a deadening complacency. Worldview formation, however, only occurs within the context of community. I would like to acknowledge here the contribution of many friends to the development of the ideas in this book. Specifically I would like to thank Mark and Metha Hines, Jennifer Harris, Tom Wright, Sylvia Keesmaat, Byron Borger, Jim Olthius, Nik Ansell and Henk Hart for their encouragement and support, often through hard times. Beth Bogard provided invaluable editorial assistance. Steve Bishop and Christopher Droop from The Regius Press have been most supportive of an author who is often slow to get a manuscript complete. And finally, I want to express my thanks and love to my son, Jubal. Jubal accompanied me when various parts of this book were presented. Such 'adult talk' isn't too exciting for a ten year old, but Jubal handled those situations with all the grace and patience that could be expected for a child of his age. Fortunately our life together is also filled with things like dancing to 'rap music', playing catch and hanging out in cold hockey arenas. For these things, and for all the other ways in which Jubal fills my life with joy, I am deeply thankful.

1

On imaging God in Babylon

Christianity as a subversive cultural movement

If someone were to ask you to characterise the place of Christianity in Western culture, I wonder whether 'subversive' would be the first word to come to your mind. For example, are corporate executives, who happen to be Christian, viewed as being somehow subversive in the functioning of their corporations? Are politicians who are Christians perceived as a national security threat? Does Scotland Yard, the Royal Canadian Mounted Police or the FBI regularly monitor the worship activities of Christian churches? I suspect not.

Listen to Nobel prize winning economist Milton Friedman:

> Few trends could so thoroughly undermine the very foundations of our free society as the acceptance by corporate officials of a social responsibility other than to make as much money for their stockholders as possible. This is a fundamentally subversive doctrine.[1]

What Friedman is saying here is that anyone who believes that corporations have social responsibilities that are more foundational than the making of profits, and could even militate against the making of 'as much money as possible' for their stockholders, is propagating a subversive doctrine that could undermine 'the very foundations of our free society'. It seems to me that a Christian economic perspective would propagate precisely such a doctrine.[2] Therefore, Christianity is subversive—at least in Friedman's terms. And I think that Friedman is right.

I could demonstrate this subversive quality of Christianity in reference to any number of issues or dimensions of our secular culture, but because I want to talk about what it means to image God, I will illustrate my point primarily as it speaks to our work lives.[3] When a community in a capitalist society insists that labour—the work of our hands, the toil of our brow—is *good*, it is being subversive. Why? Because when such a community breaks with the dominant utilitarianism, which sees work as a disutility and consumer goods as utilities, it thereby breaks with the whole movement of twentieth-century industrial capitalism. This movement has propelled us into energy and capital intensive production processes which produce more and more goods at an ever increasing rate, while also decreasing the quality of the products, decreasing the role of human labour, and decreasing the resources of creation. When that is the fundamental movement of a culture, then a community which says that work is *good* and more and more consumer goods and services is *not* necessarily good, that community is being subversive. Insisting that work is an integral dimension of human life (*not* to be contrasted as productive activity over and against consumptive leisurely activity), that it is a form of worship, that it is meant to ennoble humankind, that it should be dedicated to serving one's neighbour and the stewardly care of the creation—all of these are subversive ideas.

But Christianity is not only subversive in a culture such as ours; it is also deeply offensive to the dominant forces in our culture. This offence is related to what the Bible calls 'the offence of the cross'. A Christian worldview, a Christian lifestyle lived in the light of the events of Easter, proclaims that the true lord of history is the crucified and risen one—the one who proclaimed that the kingdom of God is at hand. And that kingdom, that rule, undermines all other pretentious kingdoms and all other cultural experiments that are not rooted in the kingdom of God. This kingdom calls for their total redirection. This is a gospel that is subversive and therefore, for those who benefit from present socio-cultural arrangements, offensive.

The Christian community and worldview conflict

What is at stake in our struggle for an integral Christian witness in a secular culture? What is at stake when we propose alternative views of what labour is all about, complete with alternative understandings of the role and function of the business enterprise, alternative views of corporate social responsibilities, different structures for labour/management/stockholders/consumer relationships, and fundamentally new criteria or norms to govern all of this? What is at stake in this context *is not simply* the ability to adjust and tinker in different ways with the economic machinery of our society. From a Christian perspective, what is at stake is much more profound. To use the language of Paul at the end of his letter to the Ephesians, making such proposals, and attempting to be a Christian witness in the workplace, is to enter into nothing less than a spiritual conflict.

> For we are not contending against flesh and blood, but against principalities, against the powers, against the rulers of this present darkness (Eph 6:12).

What is at stake here are fundamental allegiances—loyalty to different gods.

Another way to say this is that Christians live out of a *worldview* or a vision of life, that is different from the worldview that dominates Western culture as a whole. Simply stated, Western culture, like any cultural experiment in history, is rooted in an underlying and unifying worldview. That worldview, like all worldviews, tells a story. The Western story is the myth of progress. This myth, which is the implicit religion of Western culture, sees history, beginning way back with Egypt and Greece (not India and China!), as a story of cumulative development leading up to modern Western society.[4] We are the culmination of the story. This story, this Western cultural myth, proclaims that progress is inevitable, if we only allow human reason freely and scientifically to investigate our world so that we can acquire the technological power to control that world in order to realise the ultimate human good, that is, an abundance of consumer goods and the leisure time in which to consume them.

This myth of progress is engraved in our high-school textbooks, proclaimed in corporate advertising, phallically erected in our downtown bank and corporation towers, propagated in our universities, assumed by our political parties, and portrayed in the situation comedies, dramas and news broadcasts on the popular media.[5] This myth idolatrously reduces human labour to the efficient exercise of power to produce maximum economic good. Serving the three gods of scientism, technicism and economism, our work lives (in both the shop and the office) are subjected to *scientific* analysis by industrial engineers and a whole army of consultants, to determine the most efficient way to accomplish the task at hand using the best and quickest *techniques* to attain the highest possible *economic* good.

It is in the context of this idolatry that we are called to be a Christian witness, because this economistic worldview does not just guide industry, the media, and government in our society. More foundationally this is the worldview that captivates the *imagination* of our society. We experience our lives in its terms. Looking at life with this worldview is as natural as breathing for us. Because, after all, it is in the air everywhere, and the church provides no gas mask.

Because this worldview defines reality for our life we simply *assume* that progress in science, technology and economics is our historical destiny. We simply *assume* that labour is a sellable commodity. We simply *assume* that labour relations are adversarial and that the stockholders own the enterprise. We simply *assume*—it is self-evident, it needs no justification—that the goal of our labour is to raise our standard of living and that this standard can be measured by a growth in the GNP, by an increase in consumptive goods and the leisure time to consume them. And all of these assumptions are rooted in fundamental beliefs about the world we live in as 'a planet for the taking'—as resources waiting for exploitation—and beliefs about who we are as human beings and what our goals in life should be—*homo economicus*!

In my judgment, these assumptions have to do with the principalities and powers with which we must contend. Indeed, it seems to me that our experience is in many ways not unlike the experience of exile for the Jews in sixth-century BC. We live in Babylon. Babylonian definitions of reality, Babylonian patterns of life, Babylonian views of labour and Babylonian economic structures dominate our waking and our sleeping. And, like the exiled Jews, we find it very tempting to think that all of this is normal. This is the way life basically should be. Western materialistic affluence coupled with two thirds world poverty is normal. A proliferation of cheap and useless consumer goods is normal. Environmental collapse is normal. Dedicating one's life to economic growth is normal. People living for the weekend is normal. A throwaway society is normal. Deficit financing is normal. Rapid and greedy resource depletion is normal. But Canadian poet and songwriter Bruce Cockburn tells us at this point that 'the trouble with normal is it always gets worse'.[6]

If our presence in this culture is to be *Christian* we must recognise with Christian insight the profound *abnormality* of it all. This means that we cannot allow our experience of exile to define reality for us. We must not allow the Babylonian economistic worldview so to captivate our imaginations that its patterns, its views, and its priorities become normal for us.

This was also the central problem for the exiled Jews in Babylon. One of the ways in which they dealt with this problem was by constantly reminding each other of who they really were. In the face of Babylonian stories and myths, Jews told and retold their own stories. In fact, it was most likely at this time that they first wrote down one of their most foundational stories—the creation story.[7] Since we live in a culture that tells a different story—a progress story with *homo economicus* as the Promethean hero—and since that story so often captivates our imagination, it seems to me that we should never tire of re-telling to each other that very same creation story. We must allow its vision of being human to captivate our imaginations and to give us direction and hope in our cultural captivity.

Called to image God: a contextual rehearing of Genesis 1:26-28

We live in an image-conscious society. Everyone is concerned about their image—how they are perceived, and how they perceive themselves. We all want to project a certain image.

This is nowhere more evident than in the political arena. Political campaigns are media events in which the real issue is never the substance of the candidates' views and policies; instead, it is the image that is communicated through well-orchestrated 'photoopportunities' that becomes the basis upon which we are asked to choose. No wonder so many of us become cynical during elections!

Sixth-century Babylon was into images in a big way.[8] According to Babylonian mythology there were two kinds of people—those who were the spitting images of the gods, and those who were not. Those who were not the images of the gods were the slaves of the gods.

All of this goes back to the Babylonian creation story, called the *Enuma elish*.[9] According to this story a battle took place in the Babylonian pantheon of the gods way back at the beginning of history. One of the gods, named Marduk, engaged in a battle to the death with the sea goddess Tiamat, who, with the encouragement of her lover god Kingu, attempted a coup d'état in the pantheon of the gods. Marduk killed Tiamat and cut her body in half. Not knowing what to do with the body, he used the top half to create the sky and the heavens and the lower half to create the earth. But Marduk still needed someone to populate the earth and tend to its upkeep, so he created human beings out of the blood of the other dead god, Kingu.

Given this story of how humans were created you can guess what kind of value human life had in Babylon—not much! But even worse than *how* humans were made was *why* humans were made. Richard Middleton comments on this Babylonian mythology: 'You see, after Tiamat had been slaughtered and the world made, it seems that the other defeated and demoted gods had too much hard work to do, too much menial labour. So Marduk created human beings as cheap slave labour to do the dirty work of the lower gods.'[10] And to make sure that the gods did not have to pollute themselves by having too much to do with these slaves, these products of the blood of Kingu, Marduk ordained certain people—people like the high priest, the king and princes, the priests and priestesses and the lords and ladies of the high court—to be the *images* of the gods on earth. Where these people (the royal bearers of the image of the gods) could not be, idols would be erected and the idol would image the god to the people.[11]

So there were two kinds of people in Babylon. When the élite of the land looked into the mirror they would see a veritable god! These people would simply exude divinity! Marduk and the other gods would rule through them. But what would anyone else see when they looked in the mirror? They would see a nobody—an insignificant, expendable nobody—a mere slave of the gods.

You can imagine which group of people the exiled, conquered, dejected and downtrodden Israelites belonged to—they were at the bottom of the rung of the ladder of nobodies. They weren't even Babylonian slaves! They were a vanquished people, surrounded by the Babylonian élite—the powerful Babylonian movers and shakers—the Babylonian images of the gods. Being taken from their land reduced them to non-persons, stripped of all cultural power and robbed of their identity. And to make all of this worse, these Jews had a sneaky suspicion that it was precisely their God—Yahweh—who had sent them into this exile, this God-forsaken captivity. A once proud, flourishing people—a people that other nations were jealous of because of the power and vitality of her covenantal relationship with Yahweh—was now reduced to a smouldering stump, a servile people in a foreign land.

It was in this context that someone was inspired by God to write down the story that had been told by parents and grandparents for generations, the story we have in Genesis 1, the creation story. Genesis 1 is written to despairing exiles to give them hope. It cuts through the experience of exile to ground life in something more fundamental than the Babylonian experience—the creation itself. And it provides hope in a Babylonian context by being a well-crafted, probably liturgically enacted critique of that whole Marduk, Tiamat, and Kingu story of creation.

Creation, says Genesis 1, is not the result of some bloody battle between petty gods in the Babylonian pantheon! It is not formed out of the carcass of some defeated sea-monster named Tiamat! Rather, it is the result of the loving, calling Word of God. God wills the creation into being. God evokes the creation, calls the creation. Creation, then, is, in its very being, a response, an answer to the Creator's call.

You see, writing that story down and proclaiming it in worship in the context of Babylon is not simply an exercise in comparative mythology or a suggesting of an alternative understanding of how creation got started. Rather, telling this story is a subversive act. It says, in the face of a powerful and brutal empire, that the true God of creation, the true lord and sovereign, indeed, the only king, is none other than Yahweh, the God of these vanquished Israelites. He, not the body of Tiamat, is the source of creational life. And he, not Marduk or his underlings, is the final rule, power and authority in heaven or on earth. To tell this story is to engage in an act of radical civil disobedience because it dethrones, dismantles and topples the false god Marduk. To tell this story liberates a people in captivity by liberating their imaginations. This story gives them an alternative worldview, an alternative reality.

Having dismantled the Babylonian creation myth, it is not surprising that the story goes on to liberate Israelite self-understanding and to provide the exiles with a radical alternative to the Babylonian view of human life.

> Then God said, 'Let us make man in our image, in our likeness, and let them rule over the fish of the sea and the birds of the air, over the livestock, over all the earth, and over all the creatures that move along the ground.' So God created man in his own image, in the image of God he created him; male and female he created them. God blessed them and said to them, 'Be fruitful and increase in number; fill the earth and

subdue it. Rule over the fish of the sea and the birds of the air
and over every living creature that moves on the ground (Gen
1:26-28).

It seems to me that this text, which must undoubtedly be at the
very foundation of any attempt of ours to be a Christian community in a secular culture, is one of the most radical texts in
the Bible. In the context of Babylonian exile this text says that
it is not the élite, the rich and powerful in Babylon—those who
hold the keys to sacred knowledge, those who wield political
power—who are the image of God. Rather, ordinary human
beings, men and women in partnership, image God in the
creation.

Try to imagine the liberating impact of this text as it must
have been heard by Israelites who had no power, no control, no
land, no identity, no room in history to be culture-formers, and
who had been told that it is precisely their oppressors, their
captors, who are God's image-bearers. And then they hear that
they are created and called to be the image of God.[12] Against all
the odds, against all empirical evidence, indeed, against all the
principalities and powers (the *imperial* evidence!), these insignificant, broken people now have an identity. They are *not* slaves,
not expendable cheap labour, *not* the subjects of the gods of their
exilic existence, but rather they are nothing less than children of
the Creator God, the bearers of the divine image.

The closest analogy today would be to say in apartheid-
ruled South Africa that 'black is beautiful'. That does not give
blacks the vote. It doesn't immediately transform a situation of
injustice into one of community and justice, but it does liberate
and empower an oppressed and powerless people. Genesis
1:26-28 did this in sixth-century BC Babylon. It smashes the
mirror of the élite who see a veritable god staring back. And it
smashes the mirror of the ordinary person—Jew or Babylonian—who sees a nobody, a slave, staring back.

To be created in the image of God is, in the first place, a
blessing—'and God blessed them and said...'—and it occurs in
a context of creation as a blessed reality, a reality that is fundamentally affirmed—'it is good, it is good, it is good'. For

human beings to exist in creation and to be busy with creational tasks—that is, to work—is good. It is a blessing, not a curse, not a necessary evil, not a subjection of slavery to the gods, whether that be Marduk or technical power or economic growth.

This passage radically affirms human labour. What we do is not worthless or meaningless. Nor will we find worth or meaning by doing our work in the service of false gods. Our work is affirmed as worthy and meaningful when it is done in stewardly service of the Creator.

There is, therefore, in this blessing and affirmation a fundamental imperative, a foundational command, a cultural mandate. But this imperative, command and mandate must always be heard in the context of blessing and affirmation. Creation lives a gifted existence.[13] Its very being is a gift of the Creator. Human bearers of the divine image are also gifted. With every gift there is entailed a task, an appropriate response, a responsibility. The task of God's image-bearers, says this text, is to *rule* the creation. Indeed, that rule is to be in the name of the Creator-King. That rule and the power which is the office of the ruler is to be exercised as the Creator-King exercises his rule and power. In the context of Genesis 1 it is clear that such power is exercised to evoke, call into being, and bless the creation. This is a rule which is the direct opposite of a destroying, exploitive use of power. We are called, as male and female, equal co-partners in our labour, to be stewards of the creation: to use human culture-forming power to open up the creation, rather than to close it down, and to evoke new possibilities of creativity, justice, care and fulfilment rather than to close life down to those possibilities.[14] That is why one of the common images in the Bible for both God and his servants is that of the shepherd-king—a king who has dominion, but who exercises that dominion by protecting his creational subjects.

As stewards of the creation we recognise that its ownership resides with God and that we are accountable, in the final analysis, to the Creator for our use of the creation. Therefore we confess that any wanton misuse or destruction of creation—whether the good creational gifts of land, plants, water, air and atoms, or aesthetic life, family and scholarship—is a misuse of our stewardship, a squandering of our creational inheritance, and, therefore, a sin to the creation, to future generations, and ultimately to the Creator himself.

As God's image-bearers we are given the royal task of being creational gardeners. We are called to till and to keep our creational home—to open up the creation, to make it fruitful, to protect and to love it.

For Christians, the supreme example of what Genesis 1:26-28 means is found in Jesus Christ—he who is the perfect image of God, the new Adam, the pioneer of redeemed humanness. From Jesus we learn that our dominion, our rule, is not a matter of grasping at power, nor is it a matter of controlling reality and making reality serve us and our insatiable consumer appetites. No, this Jesus, though he was the very form and image of God 'did not regard equality with God as something to be exploited, but emptied himself, taking the form of a servant ... he humbled himself and became obedient unto death, even the death of a cross' (Phil 2:6-9).[15]

Isn't that amazing? We have come full circle. The Babylonians tell us that we are mere slaves of the gods. Genesis answers by saying that we are the very image of God. And then Jesus fills out what it means to be the image of God by becoming a servant. But there is a world of difference between being told that you are a slave to those who are the malicious image-bearers of the gods, and being told (and moreover, *shown*) by the very incarnate Son of God, that true image-bearing is being a servant. This is a servitude that is redemptive.

In the life of Jesus, and especially in his cross, we see how the New Testament provides an exegesis of Genesis 1:26-28. What does it mean to have *dominion* over the creation? It means that we follow the example of the one we call *Domine*—Lord. And what does this Lord call us to do? He calls us to pick up a cross and follow him. The cultural mandate is the call to service. The call to dominion is a call to lay down one's life for that which we have dominion over. The call to rule is the call to sacrifice one's own power and one's own gain for the sake of the other.

Reading the cultural mandate in these terms, understanding what it means to be God's image-bearers in the light of Jesus' form of dominion—which is an enthronement on a cross— would have, I suspect, far-reaching implications for a church that seeks to follow Jesus and to be renewed communally as God's image-bearers in the context of Western culture.

At the beginning of this chapter I said that the Christian community is called to be a subversive movement in Western culture. I am writing this little book to plead with you to heed this call because if we do not experience our lives as subversive forces in this culture then I fear that we will become comfortable in exile, comfortable with Babylonian definitions of reality, and with Babylonian gods. In fact, because I believe that the Christian community has already succumbed to the temptation of a comfortable exile, the issues that I raise here have a certain sense of immediacy to me. In the next chapter we will look at this problem in more depth.

Notes

1   Quoted by Edward Vanderkloet, 'Why Work Anyway?' in *Labour of Love: Essays on Work* (Toronto: Wedge Publishing, 1980), p. 34. This is an excellent book of essays on a Christian perspective in work.

2   See for example, Alan Storkey's book *Transforming Economics: A Christian Way to Employment* (London: Third Way Books and SPCK, 1986), and Donald Hay's *Economics Today: A Christian Critique* (Leicester: Apollos Press, 1989).

3   For a profound discussion of the nature of a subversive spirituality in the context of our culture see John Francis Kavanaugh, *Following Christ in a Consumer Society: The Spirituality of Cultural Resistance* (Maryknoll, New York: Orbis Books, 1981).

4   According to one of the most recent proponents of this myth, this story of Western intellectual, technological and economic progress is nothing less than 'the common ideological heritage of mankind'. The implication, of course, is that cultures that have not historically been animated by this particular myth (which includes most of the world's cultures until very recently) are arrogantly excluded from this common ideological heritage. See Francis Fukuyama, 'The End of History?', *The National Interest* (Summer, 1989), p. 9. I will

evaluate and critique Fukuyama's position in some detail in Chapter 3 of this book.

5   I have addressed this myth at greater length in the book I co-authored with J Richard Middleton, *The Transforming Vision: Shaping a Christian Worldview* (Downers Grove: IVP, 1984), chs 8 and 9, and in my inaugural lecture *Who Turned Out the Lights? The Light of the Gospel in a PostEnlightnment Culture* (Toronto: Institute for Christian Studies, 1989). I will also return to these issues in the next chapter.

One of the most important works on the progress ideal in Western society is Bob Goudzwaard's *Capitalism and Progress: A Diagnosis of Western Society*, translated by Josina Van Nuis Zylstra (Toronto and Grand Rapids: Wedge and Eerdmans, 1979). I have also found helpful Langdon Gilkey, *Society and the Sacred: Toward a Theology of Culture in Decline* (New York: Crossroad, 1981).

6   'The Trouble With Normal' © 1983 Golden Mountain Music Corp. Words and music by Bruce Cockburn. Taken from the album *The Trouble With Normal*. Used by permission.

7   This is not to say that the Hebrews had no creation story before the Babylonian exile. Nor is it to engage in speculation concerning when the actual story of Genesis 1-3 became current in Israel. Indeed, since the exposition that follows depends heavily on mythical parallels and contrasts with the Babylonian story, it is also worth noting both that the Babylonian myth is itself of significant antiquity, certainly pre-dating the exile, and that the Hebrew creation story could also be read as a polemic against Egyptian mythology. The strongest historical and exegetical point that I am making here is that the story was probably written down during the exile and that it functioned subversively in that context. Consequently, this exposition does not preclude the antiquity of the first chapters of Genesis.

8   I am deeply indebted to an unpublished sermon called 'Dancing in the Dragon's Jaws' written by my friend Richard Middleton for any insight that this exegesis might contain. Any errors I take full responsibility for.

See also Allen Verhey's sermon, 'In Praise of the Mighty and Creative Word', *Reformed Journal* 40 (No 4) (April, 1990), pp. 9-11.

9   Bernhard Anderson's classic book, *Creation Versus Chaos: The Reinterpretation of Mythical Symbolism in the Bible*, 2nd edn (Philadelphia: Fortress Press, 1987) is an excellent discussion of the relation between the biblical view of creation and the Babylonian worldview. For a more philosophical description of the Babylonian

myth, see Paul Ricoeur, *The Symbolism of Evil*, translated by Emerson Buchanan (Boston: Beacon Press, 1967), pt II, ch. 1. For further discussion and a translation of the *Enuma elish* see Alexander Heidel, *The Babylonian Genesis: The Story of Creation*, 2nd edn (Chicago: University of Chicago Press, 1951).

10 Middleton, 'Dancing in the Dragon's Jaws', *op. cit.*, p. 4.

11 The evidence for this identification of the king and, by extension, other members of the royal court, as the 'image' of the gods is widespread throughout ancient near eastern cultures, including Babylon, though is not attested to in the *Enuma elish* itself. For further discussion of this see D J A Clines, 'The Image of God in Man', *Tyndale Bulletin* 19 (1968), pp. 80-5.

12 For further discussion of the notion of the image of God see my *The Transforming Vision*, pt 2, and Douglas John Hall, *Imaging God: Dominion as Stewardship* (Grand Rapids and New York: Eerdmans and Friendship Press, 1986).

13 Walter Brueggemann also addresses the gifted character of creational life in *The Land: Place as Gift, Promise and Challenge in Biblical Faith* (Philadelphia: Fortress Press, 1977).

14 For further discussion of the nature of stewardship, see Wesley Granberg-Michaelson, *A Worldly Spirituality: The Call to Take Care of the Earth* (San Francisco: Harper and Row, 1984); and Loren Wilkenson *et al*, *Earthkeeping: Christian Stewardship of Natural Resources* (Grand Rapids: Eerdmans, 1980).

15 Cf. Tom Wright's chapter on this passage in *Climax of the Covenant: Christ and the Law in Pauline Theology* (Edinburgh and Minneapolis: T & T Clark and Augsburg/Fortress, 1991), ch. 4.

2

Beyond worldview to way of life: diagnosis

A worldview/way of life gap

In the last chapter I began to sketch out, in the context of an interpretation of Genesis 1:26-28, a vision for Christian cultural witness in a secular culture. I suggested that the biblical perspective of human beings as God's stewardly image-bearers is best understood when read in the context of Babylonian exile and Babylonian mythology. For us to be liberated to image God in our cultural context also requires a sensitive and discerning reading or diagnosis of that culture. This is one of the purposes of this chapter. But before we can discern the spirits in our culture we must engage in some self-critique, some discerning of ourselves. Our analysis of Babylon must be intimately related to an analysis of where we are as a Christian community exiled in Babylon.

I want to be very personal and very clear in what I say in this chapter. I feel, and I suspect that most of us feel, a gap in our lives: a gap between our worldview and our way of life. Or to put this in more biblical terms, most of us sense a gap between our conscious commitment to Jesus Christ and the way we live out our lives.

This gap creates a crisis of credibility in our relationships with non-Christians when they legitimately ask us whether following Jesus makes any difference in our lives—because, as far as they can see, it does not. This creates a crisis of integrity for those of us in the church. Indeed, the gap creates a spiritual crisis that leads many sensitive Christians to abandon (at best) the church, or (at worse) the faith altogether.

In his book, *Fragmented Gods*, Canadian sociologist Reginald Bibby has documented this gap in the Canadian churches. He sums his argument up well when he says:

> Canadians who are religiously committed [and here he is referring primarily to Christians of all denominational perspectives] construct reality in much the same manner as others. They relate with neither more nor less compassion. They experience a level of well-being that is neither higher nor lower than other peoples.[1]

What Bibby says of Canada is, I suspect, equally applicable throughout what was once called Christendom, certainly including the United States and the United Kingdom. If Bibby's analysis is right—if Christians, all of their idiosyncratic religious doctrines notwithstanding, really do construct reality in pretty much the same terms as everybody else; if, in fact, they relate to immigrants, single mothers, the poor, the handicapped and anyone else who is 'different' with neither more nor less compassion than others; and if they really do experience social, emotional and economic well-being in the same terms as everyone else in our culture—then we are faced as a church and as individual Christians with a spiritual crisis of mammoth proportions.

If all of this is true, then we are in a situation where we have to ask ourselves whether our Christian faith, our allegiance to Jesus, has any integrity at all. Or are we simply mouthing pious words and going through pious motions that betray a hollow faith? The question that we must ask is this: does our worldview—even a well-articulated, comprehensive transformational worldview—give rise to a restorative, healing, redemptive and therefore culturally subversive way of life, or doesn't it? If we are not prepared to consider that question then perhaps we are better off simply maximising our economic potential in the marketplace instead of wasting our time reading (and writing) books like this one.

Another way to consider this question is to ask whether Theodore Roszak was right when he said that the piety of

Christians is 'socially irrelevant, even if privately engaging'.[2] Or was Martin Luther King Jr right when he said 'that most people, and Christians in particular, are thermometers that register the temperature of majority opinion, not thermostats that transform and regulate the temperature of society'? Is it true that Christians are, by and large, culture *followers* and not culture *formers*?

I think that all of these things are true. The reason for this state of affairs—nothing less than a spiritual catastrophe in the Western church—is, I submit, the *enculturation* of the church. As a community of believers and as individuals we have, mostly against our best intentions, been thoroughly sucked in to our secular culture. This is what I mean by the term 'enculturation'. Our consciousness, our imagination, our vision has been captured by idolatrous perceptions and ways of life. The dominant worldview, the all-pervasive secular consciousness, has captured our lives. And what is so intriguing about this phenomenon is that we were not taken after a long drawn-out fight. No, it happened in our sleep. You see, while we were fighting with each other about evolution, the infallibility of the Bible, spiritual gifts, and various other hotly debated issues, we were falling into a deeper and deeper sleep in relation to the cultural captivity of our very consciousness. We were asleep to the secularisation of our lives and of our most fundamental values. We simply bought into the materialistic, prestige oriented, secular values of our age without ever noticing that that is what was going on. This is what Os Guinness, in his creative and provocative book *The Gravedigger File*, calls 'the Sandman Effect'. He writes, 'Instead of the church becoming more and more alert as cultural danger approaches, she falls into a deeper and deeper sleep.'[3] At present, the church is virtually in a coma, asleep to her own cultural entrapment.

It doesn't take too much cultural insight to see how this is devastatingly true in certain circles of evangelicalism that simply identify affluent capitalism with the gospel. But can it also be true of those of us who reject such a synthesis of the gospel with middle class comfortability? After all, don't we espouse a *transforming* vision?[4] Isn't our worldview one which affirms the lordship of Christ over all of life and insists that the battle line between the kingdom of God and the kingdom of darkness permeates everything? The answer, of course, is yes. This is our worldview and it should, in principle, guard against such enculturation.   But we know that this worldview is no simple immunisation shot that somehow protects us from what the rest of the church has experienced. We feel as if we too are caught. We too feel the worldview/way of life gap in our lives. Now the question is: why?

The first answer to this question leads us to the problem of dualism—that perverse way of looking at life that effectively splits life into two realms, one religious, the other secular. This severely limits the power, the *dunamis* (or, the 'dynamite') of the gospel to a very narrow dimension of life, leaving the rest of life open to the spirits of the age.[5]   However, nobody these days wants to be labelled a dualist. Everyone talks about the integration of faith and life, faith and learning, faith and politics, faith and work, etc. Yet the enculturation of the church continues and we feel its deathly grip in our own lives. So the question remains: why, if we are so self-consciously anti-dualistic, do we still see a split in our lives? I think that there are two reasons for this pervasive problem. The first is relevant to all Christians, the second speaks perhaps more specifically to Christians who hold a particular perspective.

While this sense of a gap between the way things are and the way things ought to be is universal, it seems to manifest itself in dualistic form for Christians for a particular reason. This reason is even more fundamental than the often acknowledged historical influence of Greek thinking in the history of the church.[6] Perhaps we Christians tend toward dualism precisely because the claim of our sovereign Lord is so radical, so all-encompassing, indeed, so total. Before such a God, dualism seems like a safe place. This God wants too much. If only we could limit his divine claim on our lives, if only we could domesticate God a little, so that he wouldn't make such embarrassing claims on us. Such a limiting domestication of God is the stuff of which dualism is made. While a split life is disinteg-rated and not whole, it is *more comfortable* than the radical obedience that might entail a cross, *more safe* than a discipleship that calls us to risk all for Jesus sake. Perhaps we are like the schizophrenic who feels secure in his schizophrenia and for whom healing is terrifying.

But there is a second reason for the persistence of dualism amongst people who espouse a 'transforming vision' and who have been influenced by a reformational perspective.[7] I men-tion this with some hesitation. Could it be that the form of our dualism, the particular character of a reformational faith that buys into the universal Christian problem of dualism, is that our worldview is primarily conceived in terms of intellectual cat-egories? Could it be that our problem (and trust me when I say *our* problem, I mean it) is intellectualism? It seems to me, all of our criticism of rationalism aside, the reformed tradition is guilty of over-intellectualising Christian faith.[8]

Remember here that this is a professor writing these words. Intellectual reflection is my bread and butter. So please do not hear what I am saying as anti-intellectual. What I am concerned with is not intellectual activity *per se*, but with intellectual*ism*— that is, the intellectualisation of Christian faith to such a degree that professing Christ becomes a matter of saying 'I do' to a system of theological dogmas rather than 'I do' to a bridegroom named Jesus who wants to enter into a relationship of passion-ate covenant-keeping with you and me.

The intellectualistic rubber hits the road in relation to the questions we are addressing when we consider the unexamined assumption that *right thinking* necessarily leads to *right acting*. I want to suggest to you that there is no evidence—no evidence whatsoever—that this is the case. Getting our conceptual cat-egories right is no guarantee that an integral and restorative lifestyle will follow.

Could it be that we experience this worldview/way of life gap in our lives because we have so over-intellectualised our worldview? Could it be that while our thought categories are self-consciously Christian and articulated in clear reformational terms, our way of life has been left open to enculturation? Or to put the question differently, could it be that while we have been intellectually attuned and awake we have been culturally asleep? Could it be that because we have so intellectualised our worldview our *imagination* has been taken culturally captive? Could it be that our faith is intellectually engaging, but still culturally irrelevant?

You see when we simply *assume* that the primary role of government is to enhance economic growth, that the world will always consist of haves and have-nots, that schooling has to do with discipline, skill and the acquiring of information, that the ultimate issue in the abortion debate is the conflict of women's and fetal rights, that there is something normal about what we see on television, and that good business has to do with making the right connections in order to maximise profits—then the very presence of those assumptions in our daily living and our essential inability really to imagine that all of this might be abnormal, a profound distortion of our lives, is an indication that our imaginations have been taken captive by the dominant consciousness. We can't really imagine life being any other way. I suggest to you that when it comes right down to it we have, in practice, adopted a non-Christian worldview because one's worldview is more fundamentally concerned with one's socio-cultural and historical imagination then with one's intellectual categories. And *this*, I believe, is the most perilous danger of a community influenced by a reformed perspective: that its intellectualisation of its own worldview leaves it open to the enculturation of its imagination.

There are two other reasons why our imaginations might succumb to the temptation of enculturation. Both of these reasons are very important, but I will mention them here with little elaboration.

First, an intellectualistic worldview tends to be static, encased in categories of timeless truths. This means that there can be little dynamic interplay between this worldview and the way of life that it supposedly spawns.[9] Conflicts and tensions in our cultural day to day lives are not allowed to touch our worldview. We do not allow the reality of our lives to inform or correct our worldview.

The second problem follows upon this and could well merit a whole book to discuss it properly. Just as an intellectualistically conceived worldview is static, not dynamic, so also is the God who is at the centre of that worldview static, not dynamic. Could it be that we can't imagine our cultural reality to be radically different because we can't really imagine God *doing anything*? Could it be that the God who we know as the dynamic God of history has become the passive keeper of timeless doctrinal truths and has, thereby, ceased to be *active* in history? Could this be why we do not really expect God to be active in our history?[10]

Remember that what I am attempting to offer in this chapter is a *diagnosis* of our present situation. I have begun by addressing the worldview/way of life gap in our lives, the problems of intellectualism and enculturation, and the captivity of our cultural imaginations. Before proceeding to further diagnosis of our cultural context I think that it is important to reflect for a moment on the nature of the diagnosis we are engaging in here.

The nature of the diagnosis

The crisis of credibility and integrity that we have identified in the church occurs in the context of a broader crisis in Western civilisation. There is something terribly wrong. What is wrong is *terribly* wrong because the problem lies in the very roots of our culture and in its fundamental direction. The interrelatedness of the problems that face us suggests that they all have a common root.[11] You see, the problems of environmental breakdown and resource depletion, deficit financing and two thirds world debt, South African apartheid and dictatorship in Latin America, abortion and the arms race, suicide, depression, incest, abuse and sexism, the crisis of agriculture and the vulnerability of our economic system, together with the failure of the welfare state, are all interrelated. Solving any one of these problems will not be possible without understanding this. These are all symptoms of an underlying disease, and if we address the symptoms without addressing the disease then we end up perpetrating the very infection we seek to cure.

The question becomes: what kind of diagnosis (and therapy) do we need? And to answer that question we can get a clue from the kind of language that people use when the symptoms become acute. Let me give you an example. Monday 19th October 1987—the day that the world stock markets went into a tail spin and crashed—has been dubbed 'Black Monday'. A *Time* magazine article, entitled 'After the Fall', states that the 80s ended on Monday 19th October 1987.[12] The stock market wasn't the only thing that crashed. Illusions of financial security crashed, *Reaganomics* (and its sister, *Thatcheromics*) crashed. *Time* says, 'Now it's the morning after, and the dream of painless prosperity has been punctured.'[13]

So the crash is a symptom of the destruction of false dreams. But what is the nature of those dreams? The headlines in the papers on that day give us a further clue. In Canada the largest daily carried this headline: **ARMAGEDDON!** To convey a sense of the significance of these incomprehensible events on the floors of stock exchanges around the world, journalists resorted to apocalyptic language. Black Monday is Armageddon! This is, of course, an image of the end of history. If a stock market crash is symptomatic of something as apocalyptic as Armageddon, what does that tell us?

It tells us two things: first, that an event like the stock market crash has *religious* significance in our culture. It is a religious crisis that shakes us to the very roots of our cultural being. Second, it indicates where the religious roots of our culture really lie. If history ends when the stock market crashes, then the religious assumption is that economic growth is the motor of history. When there is economic growth, history moves forward. When the economy is in crisis, history is in crisis.

If this is true, then we have an indication of how to diagnose our present cultural crisis and how we can respond Christianly to that crisis. Our diagnosis is religious in character—it is a worldview diagnosis. It is a diagnosis of the state of our culture's imagination—its understanding of itself, and its vision of the future. It is a diagnosis that attends to what a culture considers to be most important in life and what is of secondary importance.

Further, since our analysis is diagnostic, we are concerned with the relative health or sickness of this cultural vision of life. Such diagnosis requires spiritual discernment that is historical in character. We need to discern the times. Where are we in our cultural history?

It is important to realise here that while this kind of diagnostic analysis will require the use of all the intellectual tools and academic disciplines at our disposal (from biology to physics, to psychology, sociology, literature, philosophy and economics), and therefore requires interdisciplinary reflection, essentially this diagnosis is *not an academic matter*. Academic reflection is indispensable to our determination of the diagnosis, but at *heart* this analysis requires a *spiritual* discernment that is not reducible to academic reflection. Instead, this discernment is the very foundation of such reflection.

If we are to discern spirits then we will need to be filled, renewed, transformed, enlightened and led by the Spirit of God. And such fullness, renewal, transformation, enlightenment and leading cannot occur apart from a profound grasp of (and being grasped by) the biblical worldview. This is what we could call a spiritually renewed imagination—an imagination that is enlightened by the Word of God. The light of the Word of God is a light to the world. It illuminates our cultural paths, or it is no light at all.[14]

To discern spirits is to know that humans, being created in the image of God, necessarily worship graven images when they turn their backs on their Creator and Redeemer. Therefore, Christian cultural discernment must be attuned to any and all forms of idolatry. It is an analysis that seeks out idols and discerns their demonic distortion of human life.[15]

Further, to engage in spiritual/cultural diagnosis requires that we have a sense of what spiritual/cultural health or wholeness looks like. For this we need wisdom. That is, we need to grasp and be grasped by the wise ways of the Lord in creation.[16]

We need to know deeply and intimately the *wisdom* of God—God's loving rule and healing norms and direction for our cultural life—if we are to both diagnose our present disease and prescribe healing redirection. Our diagnosis must be rooted in a normative vision.

Another way to describe the nature of the diagnosis that we are working on here is to say that we are engaging in prophecy. Indeed, when a culture is following idols, and the covenant community is asleep in its enculturation, what we need is a prophetic vision. Old Testament scholar Walter Brueggemann says that 'The task of prophetic ministry is to nurture, nourish, and evoke a consciousness and perception alternative to the consciousness and perception of the dominant culture around us.'[17] The prophet is first to *criticise* and dismantle the dominant worldview, and then to *energise* the covenant community with an alternative worldview, an alternative imagination.

As unpopular and controversial as it may seem, prophetic vision must begin with criticism. That is why God told Jeremiah that he must 'pluck up and break down, destroy and overthrow' *before* he can 'build and plant' (Jer 1:10). To nourish a prophetic vision the prophet must offer his critique with passion. Only passion can wake the church (and the culture) from its secular slumber.

To be prophetic is, in the first instance, to bring biblical, redemptive critique to the church. It is self-critique. Consequently, the prophet denies us the luxury of an us/them mentality. It is not a question simply of our culture having a sickness unto death. Insofar as we are enculturated we have the same condition. And it does appear to be terminal.

The prophet must speak with passion because the community is in a coma. Or to shift the metaphor, we are numb.[18] To be numb is to be without passion; it is the absence of pathos; it is a-pathy. We are so numb that we don't even realise what has happened to us. Our numbness denies us of a spiritually renewed imagination. We are numb, we don't notice the perverse abnormality of affluence. We are numb to the precariousness of our times, numb to the danger of the earth, to the pain of the poor, to the impossibility of our present affluent lifestyles. We are numb to our own pain, and we want to remain numb to the pain of homosexuals in our communities and to the victims of abuse and incest. And, yes, we are numbed out by the irrelevance of the church to our present cultural malaise.

To be numb is to say 'peace, peace' when there is no peace (Jer 6:14, 8:11). It is to pretend that all is well when we know that it isn't. It is to say, 'the temple of the Lord, the temple of the Lord' (Jer 7:4), or, 'but we have a growing church with a growing budget, we have the spiritual gifts, we have established Christian organisations'—as if any of these release us from our cultural captivity.

Numbness sets in when we deny our real situation. And the prophetic task is to cut through that numbness with passion and to penetrate our self-deception. Prophecy refuses to allow those who say 'peace, peace' or those who say 'the-church-is-OK-so-don't-rock-the-boat' to keep us in the perpetual numbness of a dream world where everything is OK and nothing ever changes. And the way in which the prophet breaks through this dream world is *not* by angry denunciations—that would only reinforce a new us/them mentality—but by anguish, tears and public mourning.

The prophet brings to public expression the pain of the community that numbness covers up. The prophet weeps over Judah, weeps over Jerusalem, weeps over Western culture, weeps over the church, because the prophet knows what time it is. She knows that it is ending time, that it is funeral time. She has, like Jeremiah, looked for peace but found none; looked for healing, but found only terror (Jer 8:15). Her grief is beyond healing, her heart is sick within her (8:18). She knows that 'the harvest is past, the summer is ended, and we are not saved' (8:20). She knows that the time of restoration is past. She asks the question, 'Is there a balm in Gilead? Is there a physician there?' (8:22) 'Is there a doctor in the house?' And the answer is *no*! Our question, as the church at the end of the twentieth-century, is whether the answer is no for us too.

To this point I have argued that our enculturation, our captive imaginations, our intellectualism and the gap between our worldview and way of life are spiritually untenable. But that is only half of our diagnosis. I will now briefly suggest a diagnosis of the culture that has taken us captive—the culture that provides the very air (as polluted as it may be) that we breathe.

A diagnosis of Western culture: 'The Candy Man's gone'

Prophets come in various forms and they communicate their vision and their critique in various ways. One of today's most eloquent prophetic voices is that of Canadian songwriter Bruce Cockburn. In his song, 'The Candy Man's Gone',[19] Cockburn creatively portrays the experiences of failed expectations, unpleasant surprises, ironic outcomes and shattered dreams and illusions. He tells us that these failed expectations are, ultimately, the result of a misplaced faith.

Cockburn begins with the image of taste:

Sun climbs toward high noon
Glimpse metallic off the bowl of the spoon
Sliding through the air toward parting lips
Watch the expression when the strange taste hits
Face crumples, tongue quickly withdraws
I hate to tell you but the Candy Man's gone

The anticipated sweetness, the anticipated taste, is rudely interrupted. What was expected did not materialise, so the 'face crumples' and the 'tongue quickly withdraws'.

In the second verse Cockburn moves from the image of taste, a very individual image and experience, to the image of family life:

Oh sweet fantasia of the safe home
Where nobody has to scrape for honey
    at the bottom of the cone
Where every actor understands the scene
And nobody ever means to be mean
Catch it in a dream, catch it in a song

Seek it on the street you'll find the Candy Man's gone
I hate to tell you but the Candy Man's gone

Even the hope for a safe home, a haven of understanding and mutual acceptance, turns out to be a 'sweet fantasia'. This is what people dream of and write romantic ballads about, but it not realistic because, here, too, the Candy Man is gone.

But who, or what, is the Candy Man? In the third verse Cockburn reveals his identity and the all-pervasive role that he has come to play in our lives and in our culture:

In the bar, in the senate, in the alley, in the study
Pimping dreams of riches for everybody
Something for nothing, new lamps for old
And the streets will be platinum, never mind gold
Well hey, pass it on,
Misplaced your faith and the Candy Man's gone
I hate to tell you but the Candy Man's gone

The Candy Man promises a life of abundance, wealth and 'riches for everybody'. But that promise is a dream that is sold to us by pimps. There is something prostituting about that dream, it has the flavour of harlotry. And now Cockburn doesn't just tell us that it will remain unfulfilled because the Candy Man's gone, but he identifies our relation to the Candy Man as a misplaced faith:

Misplaced your faith and the Candy Man's gone
I hate to tell you but the Candy Man's gone

It is not Cockburn's intention to spell out the details of what we've lost or the specifics about who the Candy Man is—he simply evokes the image and musically portrays the sense of loss. For the specifics we need to look to other prophets. The one who has had the most formative influence in my thinking is Bob Goudzwaard.[20]

Goudzwaard describes the cultural imagination of the West, the spiritual driving force, or worldview, of Western culture as dominated, and permeated, by a faith that believes that *progress* is inevitable if only we allow human reason freely and scientifically to investigate our world. Progress enables us to acquire the technological power necessary to control that world and bring about the ultimate human goal: economic affluence and security. This is a faith that can be described as a service to three false gods. Modern culture has entered into a covenant with an unholy trinity. Three good dimensions of creation, three good dimensions of our culture-forming tasks have been absolutised. They have been erected as idols and they demonically distort our cultural lives.[21] These three idols are *scientism* (the belief that science provides us with authoritative knowledge and functions as the omniscient source of revelation in our culture), *technicism* (the effective translation of scientific knowledge into power and control of the creation which promises us a scientific-technical omnipotence), and *economism* (the golden head of the idol that believes that a rising standard of living is the ultimate goal in life and the only route to personal happiness and societal harmony).

The question for our time is whether this unholy covenant is still tenable. Do these gods deliver on their promises? Can we continue to make the sacrifices necessary to appease them? My answer to all of these questions is a resounding no!

John Dewey once said that the visionary application of science and technology will make the wilderness blossom like a rose.[22] This secularisation of Isaiah's vision (see Is 35:1) remains unfulfilled. Indeed, it seems more often than not that serving these idols turns the natural garden into a human desert. The real wilderness today is the wilderness of human habitation, the wilderness of our own technological and economic cityscapes.

John Meynard Keynes once projected a life beyond economic necessity for his grandchildren.[23] This too has gone unfulfilled. In fact, no generation of Canadians since the Great Depression has faced more anxiety about the future than our own. I suspect that this is also true in countries like the United States and Great Britain. The cover story of the 7th September 1987 issue of *Maclean's* (a national magazine in Canada) declares, 'The social and economic projections indicate that the current generation of Canadian children is the first in this century that cannot reasonably expect a better lifestyle than their parents.' The author also comments that, 'our surveys among young people show they feel that they are blocked from attaining the brass ring of success because of their shrinking chances of finding a seat on the materialist merry-go-round'.[24] It is no wonder that young parents today no longer have the secure optimism of young parents a generation earlier. They are frightened for their children, and all the evidence suggests that their fears are well-founded.

It seems to me that we are coming to the end of something— the end of a cultural epoch, the end of modernity, the end of the secular imagination.[25] This ending will not be easy. Our modern culture will not grow old gracefully and die. We have entered into what Arnold Toynbee called 'a time of troubles'—a tumultuous period in which the possibility of cultural collapse looms on the horizon.[26] This is a dangerous time because a culture in decline will often do anything to preserve itself. Prophetic endings tend to be violent.

What kind of evidence might I produce to justify my claim that modernity is in decline? In the first instance, I need to admit that such claims are never totally verifiable. They are as much a matter of feeling and spiritual discernment as they are a matter of social scientific or historical observation. It *feels* as if we are at the end of a cultural epoch. But that *feeling* is rooted in real experiences and, I believe, valid cultural observations.

To begin with, scientism promised us omniscience. The religious and superstitious traditions of the past were replaced by the sure avenue to knowledge, the scientific method. What we have experienced, however, is that scientism in fact reduces our knowledge to that which is empirically verifiable and quantifiable, thereby closing us off from all forms of non-scientific knowing. Rapidly growing interest in a New Age consciousness, alternative ways of knowing, relating to nature, and healing, suggest that a cultural shift is afoot. A white lab coat no longer guarantees that the person wearing that lab coat is trustworthy. Instead, that lab coat is increasingly becoming a cause for suspicion.

Moreover, it is becoming increasingly clear even to some of our leading scientists that science produces numerous social and ethical problems that it cannot solve for itself. One of the reasons for this is that there is no clear relationship—no clear relationship whatsoever—between an increase in scientific knowledge within a culture and an increase in wisdom necessary to direct that knowledge and guide its use. Consequently, greater scientific knowledge and technological power can, if not coupled with increased virtue and wisdom, magnify human sin and foolishness and the lethal potential of that sin and foolishness for both human culture and the broader eco-system.[27] This leads to a second category of evidence.

The worldview of modern culture assumed that human freedom, armed with the technological power to manipulate the environment for human good, would have the wisdom to know what that good is. Nothing could be more self-evidently false. This worldview has lied to us about ourselves. It has not helped us to deal with the ambiguity, fallenness, self-centredness and bondage of the human will. More autonomous power has only served to increase our ability to devour the earth and destroy one another. Indeed, it appears that our devotion to technicism has, ironically, resulted in the *loss* of human autonomy and freedom in history.[28] Technology has taken on a fatalistic character in our lives. That which promised us omnipotence has rendered us powerless in history. Technology seems to roll on through history and humans adapt to its needs. This has been nowhere more evident than in the insanity of the nuclear arms race. Jonathan Schell has suggested that a nuclear holocaust and the consequent nuclear winter is 'the fate of the earth'.[29] While such a holocaust is literally 'unthinkable' and puts us face to face with an absolute evil, it is also clearly the contradictory result of autonomous human rationality.

But the nuclear threat is still just a threat; it has not yet materialised. There is another threat, however, that demonstrates that the decline of modernity is already a historical reality. I am talking about the environmental crisis. While the nations of the world have been cognisant of this problem for decades, and particularly in the last ten to fifteen years, the environmental destruction of the earth, despoliation of nature, urbanisation, and resource depletion has *increased*, not decreased over that period of time. This is the failure of economism, or better, this is the ironic success of economism. An expansionary economic ethic necessarily destroys the earth. An economics that knows nothing of contentment, of 'enough', necessarily sacrifices the environment (and especially the environment of others) in order to satiate its greed. It is powerless to do anything else.

Here we get to the crux of the issue of our diagnosis: the myth of economic growth, Cockburn's 'Candy Man'. Simply stated, the belief that human well-being requires higher and higher levels of consumption has been shown to be both untrue and mortally dangerous. The social statistics of any area with a high Gross National Product demonstrate the absurdity of this myth. There is no relation—no relation whatsoever—between economic wealth and personal happiness, fulfilment and well-being. Material prosperity does not bring human fulfilment or happiness. The Bible has always taught this. We are just beginning painfully to learn this lesson.

If this shows that the myth of economism is a lie, then the environmental crisis demonstrates that it is mortally dangerous. Economic growth is threatening our lives. Now perhaps we could say that living dangerously is our prerogative. We are willing to gamble that either the environment will hold up long enough or that we will create the technology to clean it up and prolong life on this planet. But this gamble is, I submit, incredibly immoral. We already know that billions of the earth's inhabitants are suffering in this bargain in order to feed our consumptive habits. We are also gambling with the lives of our own grandchildren and great-grandchildren. Remember that we began this diagnosis with Keynes's prospects for his grandchildren. Now we see that they have no prospects.

The deficit financing of our society has its parallel in the deficit financing with which we exploit nature. We are drawing from a limited account when we further deplete our resources and endanger the environment, all at the expense of future generations. It is *their* creational inheritance that we are squandering. For me this is the ultimate irony of this culture. A progress-oriented, future-facing society is robbing its own grandchildren of a healthy future. We are sacrificing our children for the sake of our own economic prosperity.

I cannot help but draw a parallel here with the Ammonite god Molech. Molech was a god who required the burnt offering of children as his sacrifice. A fire would be built inside the idol, turning it red with heat. As drummers would play as loudly as possible, parents would place their children into the molten hands of the idol. The drummers would beat their drums so loudly that no one could hear the cries of the children. Is not the god of economism like the ancient god Molech? Are we not placing our children into the hands of a devouring god? Are we not a murderous generation? It is not surprising that a society that has such a hard time coming up with ways to protect the rights of the unborn would have little consideration for the rights of those who are not yet even conceived.

In light of this analysis—this diagnosis of Western culture— I conclude that we are presently in a declining culture. We are coming to the end of a cultural epoch. We are a culture running out of energy, both literally and symbolically. The depletion of cheap and abundant fossil fuels is an appropriate metaphor for the loss of cultural power and élan in the West.[30] We are in decline because we have misplaced our faith and the Candy Man's gone. In the next chapter I will investigate this decline further, but it is important at this stage of the argument to address, at least briefly, the contours of a prophetic response.

Prophetic response

What might a prophetic response to our present cultural and personal malaise look like? Earlier in this chapter I indicated that an appropriate prophetic response to the enculturation of the church, to *our* enculturation, is not angry denunciation, but public lament and mourning. It is the passion of tears that can break through our numbness and the numbness of our culture in the face of its own decline and possible death.[31] It is only passion, that is, the capacity and readiness to feel, to suffer, to care, to have com-passion, that can cut through the emotional fat of a satiated numbness.

I want us to be a people of passion: a people who refuse to cover up our own pain and our own struggles with Christian discipleship—a people who refuse to look away from the pain of others and the pain of our culture. I am calling us to be a people who cry out in the face of oppression, who blow the whistle on lies, especially the lies we tell ourselves. Such crying out is empowering because it is addressed to one who *hears* our cry and to one who can and does *act* in response to the cry of a covenantal people.

Undoubtedly some of you are beginning to think that this has been pretty pessimistic stuff that I have been dishing out in this chapter. Perhaps you are wondering why I can't be more optimistic. Let me suggest to you that our categories ought not be *pessimism* and *optimism*, but *prophetic critique* and *prophetic hope*. Christians are not optimistic; they are people who know the ultimate source of personal, cultural and historical hope. Nor are Christians pessimistic. They are people who know that idolatry or anything else that inhibits a full-bodied, loving, covenantal obedience to God bears bad fruit in our lives, in our culture and in our history.

If we are, in fact, in a situation in which the worldview of our culture is in decline; if its cultural imagination has run dry and all it can do is mouth the old formulae about a life of prosperity for all; if that situation is exacerbated by our own captivity to the impotent imagination of our culture, then what we most desperately need is a spiritually renewed imagination. This is what Brueggemann calls a *prophetic imagination*.

You see, for a prophet, or for a prophetic community, the first question is never whether a vision or a worldview is realistic, viable, practical, implementable.[32] If that is our first question, then this is simply an indication of how our imaginations are held captive by a pragmatic, materialistic and secular culture. No, our question must be: is it *imaginable*? And whether a vision is imaginable depends upon whether the integration point of that vision, indeed, the author of that vision, can make it happen. So the question comes down to whether we can imagine a God who is not a passive observer of human affairs and world history, but a passionate participant in those affairs and that history. And if we can imagine that God could in fact be a God of history, then we would have to discern what it means for us to image that God.

Consequently, the question we must face in our political lives is whether we can *imagine* a politics of justice and compassion in place of the present politics of oppression and economic idolatry? Dare we *imagine* an economics of equality and care in place of the economics of affluence and poverty? Can we *imagine* what would happen if we began to disciple our children with a prophetic vision and imagination? Can we *imagine* our work life to be at one with our worship—an act of service and praise, not a necessary evil on the way to an affluent lifestyle? In a production oriented society where meaning and worth are measured by one's productivity in the market place, therefore defining retirement as a loss of worth and meaning, can we *imagine* what it could be like if the elderly had an indispensable role in our communities? Can we *imagine* a society which has broken through its morbid preoccupation with death and truly affirms life, not just at the fetal stage, but in all of its dimensions and stages? Is a relationship of friendship, instead of exploitation, with the rest of the creation *imaginable*? Is it *imaginable* that the mass media could be an agent of awakened social, cultural and spiritual renewal, rather than the one thing that numbs us into cultural complacency and sleep more than anything else? And is our imagination spiritually opened up enough to conceive of a business enterprise that is characterised by stewardship, environmental responsibility and real serviceability rather than profits, pollution and superfluous consumer goods?

It seems to me that, in the midst of a declining culture, these are the kinds of questions that a prophetic imagination raises for us. We are called to be a prophetic community, a prophetic people. We are called to be covenanting people, not consumers; passionate, not asleep; culture formers, not culture followers. That means, to quote Amos, that we must 'let justice roll down like waters and righteousness like an everflowing stream' (5:24). But it also means, to quote John's conclusion to his wonderful epistle, that we must 'keep ourselves from idols' (5:21).

Notes

1   Reginald Bibby, *Fragmented Gods: The Poverty and Potential of Religion in Canada* (Toronto: Irwin Publishing, 1987), p. 213.

2   Theodore Roszak, *Where the Wasteland Ends: Politics and Transcendence in a Postindustrial Society* (Garden City, NY: Doubleday, 1973), p. 412.

3   Os Guinness, *The Gravedigger File: Secret Papers on the Subversion of the Modern Church* (London: Hodder and Stoughton, 1983), p. 31.

4   To refer to my own book by that name.

5   It is this perversion of the gospel that Steve Shaw addresses in his wonderful book, *No Splits* (London: Marshall Pickering, 1989).

6   Middleton and I make such an argument in *The Transforming Vision*, ch.7.

7   I realise that not all of my readers will readily identify with the reformed tradition, though the original audiences for this material were people of such a persuasion. Nonetheless, I suspect that the problem of 'intellectualism' that I address in these paragraphs pertains to various kinds of Christians who take seriously the need to have an informed and an intelligent faith.

8   It is one of the great strengths of Steve Shaw's book that he evocatively addresses dimensions of life as diverse as the self, style and play, faith development, justice and dinner parties to give a sense of what it means to trust the whole of our lives to God. In this way he helps us to break free of our intellectualism.

9   Most helpful on the way in which worldview and life are dynamically interrelated is James Olthuis' article, 'On Worldviews', *Christian Scholar's Review* 14 (1985), pp. 153-164. (This article is available from the Institute for Christian Studies, 229 College St, Toronto, Ontario, Canada M5T 1R4.)

10   It could well be that it is precisely at this juncture that an interface between the charismatic and Reformed traditions could be most fruitful. Perhaps the charismatic experience could transform our worldviews, setting us free from intellectualism and setting our imaginations free for cultural transformation. Unfortunately, some of the most recent work on a charismatic worldview has not been overly helpful. I think particularly of John Wimber's *Power Evangelism* (New York: Harper and Row, 1986) which does not, it seems to me, really get us beyond the kind of dualism that debilitates the church.

11   No one has argued this more persuasively than Bob Goudzwaard in *Capitalism and Progress: A Diagnosis of Western Society*, translated by Josina Van Nuis Zylstra (Toronto and Grand Rapids: Wedge and Eerdmans, 1979).

12   Walter Isaacson, 'After the Fall', *Time* 130 (No 19) (2nd November 1987), pp. 18-19.

13   *Ibid.*, p. 19.

14   For an in-depth and provocative discussion of the Bible as a light for our paths see Hendrik Hart, *Setting Our Sights by the Morning Star: Reflections on the role of the Bible in Post-Modern Times* (Toronto: Patmos Press, 1989).

15   See Bob Goudzwaard, *Idols of our Time*, translated by Mark Vandervennen (Downers Grove: IVP, 1984).

16   My colleague Calvin Seerveld has reflected deeply on the nature of biblical wisdom. Some of the fruit of his reflection is published in his *Rainbows for the Fallen World: Aesthetic Life and Artistic Task* (Toronto: Tuppance Press, 1980).

17   Walter Brueggemann, *The Prophetic Imagination* (Philadelphia: Fortress Press, 1978), p. 13. Other works by Brueggemann that I have found to be most helpful are *The Hopeful Imagination: Prophetic Voices in Exile* (Philadelphia: Fortress Press, 1986); *Hope Within History* (Atlanta: John Knox Press, 1987); *Israel's Praise: Doxology against Idolatry and Ideology* (Philadelphia: Fortress Press, 1988); and *Jeremiah 1-25: To Pluck Up, To Tear Down*, International Theological Commentary Series, edited by F C Homgren and G A F Knight (Grand Rapids and Edinburgh: Eerdmans and The Handsel Press, 1988).

18   'Numbness' is also one of Brueggemann's favourite metaphors. Again, I acknowledge my indebtedness to him.

19 'Candy Man's Gone' © 1983 Golden Mountain Music Corp. Words
    and music by Bruce Cockburn. Taken from the album *The Trouble
    With Normal*. Used by permission.
        I have also discussed the work of Bruce Cockburn in my
    article, 'The Christian Worldview of Bruce Cockburn: Prophetic
    Art in a Dangerous Time', *Toronto Journal of Theology* 5 (No 2) (Fall,
    1989), pp. 170-87. (This article is available from the Institute for
    Christian Studies, 229 College St, Toronto, Ontario, Canada M5T
    1R4).

20 I have also learned a great deal from the writings of Lesslie
    Newbigin, *Foolishness to the Greeks: The Gospel and Western Culture*
    (Grand Rapids: Eerdmans, 1986), and *The Gospel in a Pluralist
    Society* (Grand Rapids and Geneva: Eerdmans and WCC Publica-
    tions, 1989).

21 Cf. Bob Goudzwaard, *Aid for the Overdeveloped West* (Toronto:
    Wedge, 1975). Middleton and I also discuss this false trinity at
    much greater length in *The Transforming Vision*, ch. 9.

22 John Dewey, *Reconstruction in Philosophy* (New York: Henry Holt
    and Co., 1929), p. 85.

23 J M Keynes, 'Economic Possibilities for our Grandchildren', in
    Essays in Persuasion (New York: Harcourt, Brace and Co., 1932).

24 Goody Teachman Gerner, 'Growing Pains', *Maclean's* 100 (No 36)
    (7th September 1987), p. 37.

25 In the next chapter I will address this ending as an end of history.

26 Cf. Arnold Toynbee, *A Study of History* (London: Oxford University
    Press), vol. I (1934), p. 53; and vol. IV (1939), pp. 1-5. Langdon
    Gilkey employs this notion from Toynbee in his article 'Theology
    for a Time of Troubles: How My Mind Has Changed', *Christian
    Century* 98 (29th April 1981), pp. 474-80. For further discussion of
    Gilkey's understanding of this 'time of troubles', see my book,
    Langdon Gilkey: Theologian for a Culture in Decline (Lanham, MD:
    University Press of America, 1991), ch. 3.

27 Cf. Langdon Gilkey, *Religion and the Scientific Future* (New York:
    Harper and Row, 1970), pp. 90-2, and *Reaping the Whirlwind: A
    Christian Interpretation of History* (New York: Seabury Press, 1976),
    pp. 259-60.

28 The dialectical relation of a humanist understanding of freedom
    and its inevitable loss in bondage is brilliantly addressed by
    Goudzwaard in *Capitalism and Progress*, especially chapter 15. See
    also Herman Dooyeweerd, *Roots of Western Culture: Pagan, Secular*

and Christian Options, translated by John Kraay, edited by Mark Vandervennen and Bernard Zylstra (Toronto: Wedge, 1979), chs 6 and 7.

29   Jonathan Schell, *The Fate of the Earth* (London, Pan Books, 1984).

30   That also seems to me to be why the Western world responded with such heavy-handed force to the aggression of Iraq against Kuwait in the summer of 1990. The issue is not primarily one of justice for the occupied peoples of Kuwait, but of the maintenance, at all costs, of the consumptive lifestyle of the West that is so dependent upon middle eastern oil.

31   I will return to the theme of grief and mourning in the next chapter.

32   Cf. Brueggemann, *The Prophetic Imagination, op. cit.,* p. 44.

3

Waiting for a miracle: Christian grief at the end of history

On the telling of time

I do not wear a watch. That isn't because I am making a statement, it is just that I have never been comfortable with a band around my wrist. So I am always in a position of having to ask what time it is. Now the question, 'what time is it?' can give rise to a number of equally valid responses. One could answer, 'it is 10:00AM'. Or one of my students, irritated that I never know what time it is, and it is in fact long past the time when we should have stopped for a coffee break, could say, with some cheek, 'it is time to get a watch'. There is more than one way to tell the time. It could be 'time to go'. For a woman past the ninth month of pregnancy it is time to give birth. For a man who is very elderly and infirm, it is coming close to the time to die.

The author of the book of Ecclesiastes fully understood the multidimensionality of time and so do each of us in the temporal rhythms and patterns of our day to day lives. There is a time for everything. In the context of our relationships we know that there is a time for embracing and a time to refrain from embracing. Sometimes touch, hugs, kisses and physical intimacy are important, necessary and appropriate. At other times it is just as important, necessary and appropriate to refrain from such embracing. There is a time to be silent and a time to speak, a time to tear down and a time to mend. Wisdom, says Ecclesiastes, is knowing which time is which.

That kind of time-telling wisdom is deeply embedded in what we might call the overall temporal orientation of a culture. J T Fraser once said that 'the *Weltanschauung* [or worldview] of an individual and of an age, that is the perception of life and concept of things preferred, is essentially a view of time'.[1] That is, inherent in all worldviews, all fundamental orientations and perspectives in life, is a view of time which is historically mediated to a culture through its founding, direction-setting stories. Consequently, 'Every culture is, to a great extent, a reflection of the temporal orientation it adopts.'[2]

Since one of the things that I want to call for in this chapter is that we enter into a period of mourning, I will illustrate my point about cultural time orientations in relation to the process of bereavement. We have seen, in this century, an acceleration in both Western bereavement processes and funeral practices. For example, in 1927, Emily Post said that the formal period of mourning for a widow was three years. By 1950, six months seemed long enough and in 1972 Amy Vanderbilt advised the bereaved that they should 'pursue, or try to pursue, a usual social course within a week or so after the funeral'.[3] You see, in our society death is final, life is for the living, the past is gone, so we have to get on with the present. Therefore, mourning—a process which seems to have little immediate material utility for the present—needs to be as short as possible.

The temporal orientation of one's worldview, then, is what tells you what time it is. It tells you if it is time for mourning and how long that time should last. It also tells you how to value such time.

A culture's temporal orientation informs more than just matters of personal mourning, however. Such an overall temporal perspective also determines the pace of industry and business; how fast a child should get through school or a student earn a degree; when we should marry, have children and buy a house. One of the ironic things about our society is that while the internal dynamics of society tend to be accelerating (especially in our computer age), many young people seem to be unconsciously rebelling against this temporal orientation by postponing many of these very things. Susan Littwin, the author of *The Postponed Generation: Why American Youth are Growing Up Later*,[4] says the baby-boom generation has come of age in a land of lowered expectations and a time of anxiety that has contributed to their tendency to put off adulthood, with its assumed responsibilities and maturity, until they become thirty-something. This phenomenon itself, I suspect, is changing the way our society understands time.

On the broadest canvas, however, a temporal orientation addresses itself to the larger, ultimate questions of history: its overall goals, where history is going. Our orientation gives us a vision for the future that functions as a foundation from which we evaluate history and our participation in it. We will interpret the events around us as successes or failures and we will decide what the history-making events are, who the history-shaping people are, and where we are in the process toward the final goal of history, in terms of the answers we give to these ultimate questions.[5]

At a conference hosted by the University of Guelph on 'Ethics in an Age of Pervasive Technology' in October of 1989, there was a basic consensus that it was time to be deeply worried about the sustainability of life on this planet, but no consensus on what this crisis demands of us. Alexander King, the President of the Club of Rome, argued that it was time for an enlightened self-interest, an evolutionarily extended ego that would consider future generations to be somehow necessary to its own survival. And, argued King, only education could facilitate such an evolutionary step.

William McNeill, a historian at the University of Chicago, confessed that since historical process is always sovereign over human purpose in history, our only hope is to erect a massive world bureaucracy to do what bureaucracies do best—slow the process down. And John Kenneth Galbraith, maintaining his liberal Keynesian faith to the end, counselled further government intervention and control of developing technologies.

All of these men agree on one thing—we live in a perilous time of profound transition. But they differ on whether it is time for a new evolutionary step, or a world bureaucracy, or more Keynesian interventionism. I confess that while I was listening to these academic leaders at the Guelph conference I became more and more agitated. What upset me was not the vacuousness of their proposals, nor their implicit allegiance to the present status quo. What left me with a sinking feeling in my stomach was their lack of passion, or better, *com*passion. There was a certain aridness to their speech. Perhaps this isn't fair, but I did not have a sense that these men wept over the precariousness of the planet that they were so competently addressing.

It's time for the silent criers to be held in love

For my sense of time I must confess that I seldom look to scholars. Perhaps what we need to help us tell the time is poets who will teach us new ways to see. As became apparent in the last chapter, the poet who I often look to for prophetic time-telling is Bruce Cockburn. This is how Cockburn tells the time in his song 'Feast of Fools':[6]

It's time for the silent criers to be held in love
it's time for the ones who dig graves for them
    to get that final shove
it's time for the horizons of the universe to be glimpsed
    even by the faceless kings of corporations
it's time for chaos to win and walk away with the prize
    that turns out to be nothing (fooled you, fooled you)

Cockburn's reading of the times is one of passionate love and prophetic reversals. What time is it? It is 'time for the silent criers to be held in love', for those who have been deeply broken or brutally oppressed to be embraced, held in security and hope. You know who they are. They are the victims of our world, those who have been abused, ignored, forgotten and robbed of freedom and dignity. The ones who aren't given the time of day, whose pain is not acknowledged because it is silent.

But, says Cockburn, if it is time for them to be held in love, then it is also time for those 'who dig graves for them'—the abusers, the ignorers, the forgetters, the victimisers—'to get that final shove'. Cockburn's prophetic reversal is biblical because those who gain the world, lose it. Prophetic blessings are always accompanied by prophetic woes. Your time is up, says Cockburn. Those who victimise become victims. The 'faceless kings of corporations', living in their world of illusion, will finally get a glimpse of the way the universe really is before chaos wins and walks away with the prize—the goal of historical progress as defined by these kings, these 'winners', these 'movers and shakers' on the historical stage—which turns out to be nothing. 'Fooled you, fooled you!'

What time is it for Bruce Cockburn? It is time for radical reversals. This is a vision of historical discontinuity, where that which is, is *not* accepted as normal, because, says Cockburn, 'the trouble with normal is it always gets worse'.

> Fashionable fascism dominates the scene
> When the ends don't meet its easier to justify the means
> Tenants get the dregs and the landlords get the cream
> As the grinding devolution of the democratic dream
> Brings us men in gas masks dancing while the shells burst
> The trouble with normal is it always gets worse[7]

Maintaining the status quo, keeping things as they are, only makes things worse because it lacks historical discernment; it fails to be attuned to the 'grinding devolution of the democratic dream'.

Cockburn's voice is not the only prophetic voice to be speaking today. In fact, I would characterise his perspective as a minority report on the signs of the times. The majority, if I read it right, sees no such discontinuities, no such reversals, no such devolution of the democratic dream. Rather, they celebrate continuity, the triumph of the normal course of history and the final historical validation of the democratic dream. Their most recent and celebrated spokesman is not a poet, but an articulate bureaucrat from the US State Department, Francis Fukuyama.

The end of history?

In the summer of 1989 Francis Fukuyama published an article in a leading neo-conservative journal in the United States called *The National Interest*. The article is titled, 'The End of History?',[8] and it created a stir not unlike that created two years earlier by Fukuyama's former teacher, Allan Bloom, when the latter published *The Closing of the American Mind*.[9] Fukuyama began appearing on talk shows, the article was serialised into a series of shorter pieces in papers around the world, 10 Downing St. requested a copy, and numerous writers criticised or editorialised its content. One might say that a whole cottage industry arose because of this article. At the risk of contributing to what I perceive to be an already inflated market, I think it is important that Christians reflect on Fukuyama's understanding of the end of history in order to clarify our own.

Fukuyama begins his article with 'the feeling that something very fundamental has happened in world history' (p. 3). In the summer of 1989, coming to the last decade of the millennium, such events as the thaw in the cold war, the spread of *perestroika* and *glasnost* in the USSR, and the breaking out of peace between the East and West all suggest that some larger historical process is at work in our time. Fukuyama has sensed that these events are not just contingent or accidental, but that they point to something essential in history.

Fukuyama states his thesis early in the article:

> ... the century that began full of self-confidence in the ultimate triumph of the Western liberal democracy seems at its close to be returning full circle to where it started ... to an unabashed victory of economic and political liberalism (p. 3).

The winner in this historical process is not simply the economic and military power of the West, but, more importantly, this historical process demonstrates the victory of the Western *idea*, evident first 'in the total exhaustion of viable systematic alternatives to Western liberalism', and second 'in the ineluctable spread of consumerist Western culture ...' (p. 3).

Now, *if* we are inclined to agree with Fukuyama's analysis, the question remains: why is this particular historical triumph identified with the end of history? Is it not likely that somewhere in the future another ideology (probably not communism!) will come along and challenge, if not defeat, liberalism? Fukuyama's answer is to say that we do not understand the magnitude of the events before us. What we are witnessing is not accidental. Rather, we are seeing nothing less than the fulfilment of the essential character, goal and purpose of history. This is the *end*, the *telos* of history. The defeat of communism and the victory of liberal democratic capitalism marks 'the end of history as such: that is, the end point of mankind's ideological evolution and the universalisation of Western liberal democracy as the final form of human government' (p. 4). Now if this is the way things looked to Fukuyama in the summer of 89, you can only imagine how the events of the winter of 89/90 in countries like East Germany, Czechoslovakia, Hungary, Romania, Poland and Lithuania would serve to confirm him in his position.

Fukuyama spells out the theoretical foundations of his historical discernment in a discussion of the great Enlightenment idealist philosopher G W F Hegel, as interpreted by the Russian emigré to France, Alexandre Kojéve.[10] Simply stated, Fukuyama opposes all forms of materialism—whether the Marxist or the *Wall Street Journal* variety. As a good Hegelian, he insists that ideas are the real driving force of history. By 'ideas' he means the 'large unifying worldviews that might best be understood under the rubric of ideology' (p. 5). And the Idea that has been driving history all along has finally produced its climactic result—liberal capitalism. Fukuyama's central theoretical point is that ideas and consciousness in general are independent of the material world. 'Consciousness is cause and not effect, and can develop autonomously from the material world; hence the real subtext underlying the apparent jumble of current events is the history of ideology' (p. 6). While the material world can serve to enhance 'the viability of a particular state of consciousness', ultimately it is consciousness that will 'remake the material world in its own image' (p. 8).

Difficult though this point may be, it is important to note an ambiguity in Fukuyama's description of consciousness. He speaks both of something called 'a particular state of consciousness', which sounds like the particular worldview or ideology of an historical people, and of consciousness which can develop independently of the real world. This is confusing because for any consciousness to be particular it must be linked to the material world at a particular place and time. If we are to give Fukuyama the benefit of the doubt, then we will need to hear his language about consciousness to refer not primarily to what particular people thought at particular times but to the unifying Consciousness (with a capital 'C'). The Idea (with a capital 'I') that has been victorious and come to actualisation in liberal democracy is not simply the particular Enlightenment notion of human rights and freedoms, but the Idea which is the essential truth of reality—a 'truth which is absolute and could not be improved upon' (p. 8).

That is why the triumph of liberalism over communism is not a contingent or accidental event in history. It is the self-actualisation of the Absolute Idea itself, and therefore the end of history. There is nowhere else to go and no more contenders for historical dominance. The Absolute Idea has now been realised. To quote an American phrase, if it ain't over until the fat lady sings, then liberal democracy is a fat lady who has sung!

What remains in this post-historical condition is a universal homogeneous state in which all prior contradictions have been resolved and all human needs have been satisfied. Since there are no more ideological battles to be contested 'what remains is primarily economic activity' (p. 5). Or as Fukuyama says: 'We might summarise the content of the universal homogeneous state as liberal democracy in the political sphere combined with easy access to VCRs and stereos in the economic' (p. 8). Indeed, 'a universal consumer culture has become both a symbol and an underpinning of the universal homogeneous state' (p. 10).

Fukuyama's point is not that we have all reached this state, only that there are no serious competitors left. As he says, '... at the end of history it is not necessary that all societies become successful liberal societies, merely that they end their ideological pretensions of representing different and higher forms of society' (p. 13). So at the end of history, the dividing line no longer runs between ideologies like liberal democracy and communism. Rather, the dividing line runs between societies that are post-historical (having reached liberal homogeneity) and those societies which remain 'very much mired in history'—which includes, of course, most of the two thirds world (p. 15). For these 'historical' societies ideological and military conflict will continue, but since the largest and most powerful states are no longer caught in the grip of history, minor skirmishes aside, we appear to be entering into the peace of a secular liberal utopia.[11]

Having *arrived* you would think that Fukuyama would be a very happy man and that we would embark upon a time of contented, consumeristic enjoyment. But no, says Fukuyama. 'The end of history will be a very sad time' because all that called forth daring, courage, idealism and imagination from people in history will no longer be necessary, 'replaced by economic calculation, the endless solving of technical problems, environmental concerns, and the satisfaction of sophisticated consumer demands' (p. 18). The end of history is sad because it is boring![12]

So what time is it for Francis Fukuyama? It is the end of history. And though the end of history may be a little sad and somewhat boring because there is so little left to do, nonetheless it is not a time for mourning, because this end is a fulfilment. History can retire with the satisfaction that, against all of the material odds, it has completed its task, realised its essential Idea, actualised Consciousness and can now receive its gold watch for a job well done. What time is it? It is time for a self-congratulatory pat on the back in a new post-historical age!

Critique of Fukuyama

It seems to me that Francis Fukuyama is a man with blinkers on. Sadly this is what we have come to expect of someone from the State Department. His discernment of the end of history is callously blind to all of the counter-evidence to his self-congratulatory, White House-affirming position. I will list just a few of these problems.

First, Fukuyama's historical perspective, like that of his mentors, Allan Bloom, Alexandre Kojéve and G W F Hegel, suffers from what Charles Taylor calls a 'glaring Western ethnocentrism'.[13] Indeed, not only does Fukuyama dismiss the cultural perspectives of societies that are still 'mired in history', he insists that Western liberal democracy is nothing less than 'the common ideological heritage of mankind' (p. 9). Consequently, the vast majority of the world's population is excluded from what he arrogantly deems a *common* heritage. My point is that this isn't just historically arrogant and narrowly ethnocentric (an odd fate for someone who claims to be perceiving the universal and essential nature of history!), but it is also an ideological form of genocide. These other 'historical peoples' hardly have a share in what humankind is really all about.

Secondly, Fukuyama fails to see that his own account of liberal capitalism's triumph points to its possible demise. Marxism is no longer a viable option, says Fukuyama, because in the ascendency of the middle class in nations like the United States and Canada, Marx's classless society has already been achieved. But recent economic trends point to the *erosion* of that middle class. In 1967 the middle class comprised 27.4% of the Canadian population. In 1986 that figure dropped to 21.5%, while both the upper and lower classes grew during the same period.[14] There are *more* rich people today. But there are *more* poor people as well, and *fewer* in the middle class. The class conditions that are, at least theoretically, the seed-bed of communism are developing in North America. These conditions might also be the fertile soil of a new form of fascism.[15]

Thirdly, this gap between rich and poor in capitalist society points to an even more fundamental contradiction. Liberalism is, for Fukuyama, first and foremost a system of law which protects the universal human right of freedom. That right is exercised first in the democratic consent of the governed and second in the exercise of economic freedom. This is what is called 'liberal democratic capitalism'. But it is only by a far stretch of the imagination that anyone could conclude that people exercise real democratic choice in a two party system such as the United States, or even the present three party system in my own country of Canada.[16]

Even if we do grant that in such a context political freedom is meaningfully exercised, its concomitant economic freedom in our society is a cruel joke. In Canada, *nine families* control more than half of the Toronto Stock Exchange; one in seven Canadians lives in poverty; in 1989 47% of the national government's income came from individual taxpayers and only 9% came from corporate taxes. In fact, in 1987 27 billion dollars in corporate profits went untaxed. These are not the only inequalities. In the United States not one of the top 800 corporations has a black chief executive officer, only one was headed by a Hispanic, and only one by a woman.[17] These statistics suggest that it is hardly time for self-congratulations.

Fourthly, the record of liberal 'post-historical' democracy is also not very good on the international front. It is not just the Ceausescus of the world who have fallen, so have the US-backed dictators like Somoza in Nicaragua, Pinnochet in Chile, the Shah in Iran, and Marcos in the Philippines. Manuel Noriega was once a US puppet. Saddam Hussein was once an ally. And this is, of course, a profound contradiction that Fukuyama cannot possibly notice if he wants to maintain either his job at the State Department or his self-congratulatory Hegelian position.

Bruce Cockburn, however, has nothing to lose in his description of what Fukuyama calls democracy:

> padded with power here they come
> international loan sharks backed by the guns
> of market hungry military profiteers

> whose word is a swamp and whose brow is smeared
>   with the blood of the poor
>
> who rob life of its quality
> who render rage a necessity
> by turning countries into labour camps
> modern slavers in drag as champions of freedom
>
> sinister cynical instrument
> who makes the gun into a sacrament
> the only response to the deification
> of tyranny by so-called 'developed' nations'
> idolatry of ideology
>
> north south east west
> kill the best and buy the rest
> it's just spend a buck to make a buck
> you don't really give a flying fuck
> about the people in misery[18]

Perhaps Fukuyama, the State Department bureaucrat, is a 'modern slaver in drag as a champion of freedom'. You see, if the capitalist West is really the bearer of the common ideological heritage of mankind, and if it is the highest self-actualisation of Absolute Consciousness, then it propagates its liberal Idea and further manifests this Absolute Consciousness in the world in a very peculiar way! But then again, maybe it is precisely Fukuyama's distinction between post-historical and historical societies that both allows and mandates such international behaviour. While post-historical societies can now live in peace and homogeneity, societies still mired in history will require further domination until they evolve into the post-historical light of liberal democracy. Marx's dictatorship of the proletariat gets replaced by the dictatorship of the post-historical—what Cockburn calls 'the deification of tyranny by so-called "developed" nations' idolatry of ideology'.

If the contradictions of liberalism that I have discussed so far are major flaws in this particular historical consciousness, then the fifth example of Fukuyama's blindness is fatal: our threatened environment. The litany of environmental crises before us is not unfamiliar: overpopulation, desertification, species extinction, ozone depletion in the upper atmosphere and an overabundance of ozone in the lower atmosphere, air and water pollution, nuclear waste, acid rain, toxic waste, deforestation, and the greenhouse effect caused by increased CO_2 emissions. Yet none of this seems to temper Fukuyama's self-congratulatory sentiments. Perhaps this is because this condition of environmental destruction is an ironic witness to the triumph of Fukuyama's worldview: an index of liberal capitalism's success is measured in the amount of acid rain it produces.

Robert Heilbroner has noted that 'expansion has always been considered as inseparable from capitalism', and 'conversely, a "stationary", non-expanding capitalism has always been considered either as a prelude to its collapse or as a betrayal of its historic purpose'.[19] Fukuyama fully understands the first part of Heilbroner's equation but must be blind to the second. If to fulfill its historic purpose capitalism must be expansionary, and if Fukuyama's view of history cannot consider the possibility that capitalism's historic purpose has been betrayed, then environmental destruction—the unavoidable consequence of Fukuyama's world wide consumer society—is, by some strange twist of liberal logic, a normal course of history. This shouldn't strike us as odd, however, considering that it was John Locke, the father of liberalism, who said that 'the negation of Nature is the way toward happiness'.[20]

But what Fukuyama misses is that the ironic outcome of liberal capitalism's expansionary consumer ethic is *not* increased individual freedom and security, but its opposite. Liberal capitalism (and its evil Enlightenment twin, state socialism) has produced an insecure world, choking on its own waste, that will require ever increasing *limits* upon human freedom and consumer acquisition in order to come to grips with its ecologically precarious future. The ever accelerating expansionary appetites of liberal capitalism is on a direct collision course with the realities of a limited and ecologically sensitive creation.

Again, I refer you to Bruce Cockburn for a more insightful perspective:

Way out on the rim of the galaxy
The gifts of the Lord lie torn
Into whose charge the gifts were given
Have made it a curse for so many to be born

This is my trouble
These were my fathers
So how am I supposed to feel?
Way out on the rim of a broken wheel[21]

When you are 'way out on the rim of the galaxy' you are at the
outer edge of something, perhaps even at its end. But Cockburn
does not perceive this end as the end of an ideological evolution
or the successful self-actualisation of an Absolute Idea. Rather,
he sees 'the gifts of the Lord lie torn'. History, for Cockburn, is
not a necessary realisation of an essential idea of freedom in
Consciousness. No, history is an arena of responsible stewardship. Gifts have been given—the gift of creation, of culture, of
human ingenuity and creativity, and, yes, the gift of freedom.
But Cockburn sees these gifts as distorted and torn. Indeed,
they now curse us. When Cockburn asks, 'so how am I supposed to feel?', you know that Fukuyama has no answer for him.

What is Fukuyama up to?

My critique of Fukuyama up to this point has only addressed
the *content* of his position. But to be complete we also have to
attend to the *form* of his argument as well. My question at this
stage goes beyond 'what is Fukuyama saying' to 'what is Fukuyama up to?', 'what form does his argument take?', and 'what
function does this kind of literature fulfill in Fukuyama's
world?'

   To help us to get a handle on these questions I turn first to
a book written twenty years ago by sociologist Peter Berger
called *The Social Reality of Religion*.[22] What I find immediately
interesting about Berger is that his understanding of human
culture forming is clearly more complex and dialectical than is
Fukuyama's. For Berger, society is a human product (not the
necessary unfolding of an Absolute Spirit) which *acts back* on its
producer. In other words, we produce society *and* it produces

us. Society is a collective process of world-building. In forming society we order the world of time, space, relationships and values in certain ways. That society, that particular objective constellation of an ordered universe, is then internalised in such a way that it comes to form the subjective structures of consciousness itself.

What is important for Berger is that human beings, in this process of internalising into their consciousness the objectified structures of society, do so not as passive, inert recipients, but as active participants. Both the structure of society and the categories of our consciousness, or worldview, are things for which we must take responsibility. There is, however, a human tendency to project our historically conditioned categories of understanding upon the universe. This is perfectly understandable because we want to be able to assume that the way we think has a relationship to reality itself, giving our worldview a validity and legitimation that goes beyond our particular historical idiosyncrasies.

Berger describes this process of projection as *cosmization*: 'the identification of the humanly meaningful world with the world as such'.[23] Further, Berger says that religion is the agency of cosmization *par excellence*. Religion legitimates the particular worldview of a culture 'so effectively because it relates the precarious reality constructions of empirical societies with ultimate reality'.[24]

The reason that I have digressed into this description of Berger's understanding of world-construction, society and religion is to show that from the perspective of Berger's sociology of knowledge, Fukuyama is engaging in nothing less than cosmization. He is projecting upon the very nature of the universe the categories of his own liberal democratic society. Fukuyama's assumption is that *of course* no normal human being would contest the legitimacy of liberalism—that would be as futile as contesting gravity! This is simply the way the world is!

So then if, in Berger's terms, Fukuyama is engaging in cosmization, then what *kind* of argument is he mounting? Berger would say that this is a religious argument. As an act of cosmization, the argument functions religiously for Fukuyama and for his readers. He is offering us a religious reading of the world and a religious telling of the time.

There is, however, a further consequence of this religious process of cosmization, says Berger. Cosmization, by relating a particular world construction to the structure of the world as such, runs the danger of forgetting that, regardless of its necessity, and even of its relative validity, any world construction, any worldview, any human consciousness, is always historically conditioned and limited. Therefore, such world constructions cannot be totally and unambiguously identified with the ultimate structure of the universe. Any such identification is what Cockburn calls 'idolatry of ideology'. Berger calls it *alienation*. The alienated individual '...forgets that this world was and continues to be co-produced by him. Alienated consciousness is undialectical consciousness'.[25] Further, alienated humans live in a world they have made as if they were fated to do so by powers outside of themselves and independent of their own world-constructing activity.

This seems to be an apt description of Fukuyama. Not only is his argument an expression of a religious consciousness, it is also an alienated consciousness because he has forgotten that liberal democratic capitalism is an Enlightenment experiment, and not an indication of the ultimate *telos* of history. Ironically, this is also a *fated* consciousness because when it comes right down to it, the so-called triumph of liberal freedom is not an accomplishment of freedom at all, but the necessary outworking of a Consciousness that supersedes human consciousness.

Taste the depth of this irony! This liberal perspective on autonomous freedom betrays itself in the actual historical outworking of its implications in the market economy, political reality, international relations and environmental despoliation. It also self-destructs in the very form of Fukuyama's idealist defense of it. Or to put it the other way around, we are both fated to freedom, and the idolatrous misdirection of our freedom fates us. Either way, we are not free!

All of this places Fukuyama in a very precarious position because he is not just some tenured academic spinning intellectual categories for the fun of it. He is a high level State Department bureaucrat. And one of the central and indispensable tasks of government is to be the caretaker and promoter of a communal vision of the future.[26] To rule and to have power is to hold forth a compelling and believable vision of the future. Without vision, a people die. Without a coherent vision of the future, the state collapses. Perhaps this is one of the central reasons why the Eastern European states so easily crumbled in the winter of 1989. So locked up in the Stalinist past, with no vision of the future, the state could not survive under the people's call for reform and a new future.

Jeremy Rifkin has said that 'images of the future are the single most powerful socialising agents in Western culture'.[27] This seems to me to be the case in any society. It is because the state generally is the custodian and even the guarantor of such a vision that the state takes on an air of the majestic and the sacred. Therefore Langdon Gilkey argues that government's most ultimate claim to legitimacy is always stated with reference to foundational myths which 'function as essential answers to the deepest, desperate questions of historical being, to human being in passage, and so ... provide the grounds for the possibility of human freedom in that passage...'[28]

What then is Fukuyama, the agent of the State Department, up to in his article on 'The End of History?'? He is the purveyor of myth. He is reflecting on the present status of the myth in terms of recent historical developments. In biblical language, he is fulfilling a prophetic ministry because it is always the office of the prophet to tell what time it is, and to direct the community into the future.

Fukuyama meets Jeremiah

A time in the biblical period that is analogous to our time because of the sense that momentous changes were on the near horizon of world history is the period that ran from the end of the seventh-century BC (say from the death of Josiah in 609) to the fall of Jerusalem in 587. In the North the Assyrian empire was abruptly replaced by the Babylonians under the rule of Nebuchadnezzar, and the Babylonians had clear expansionist intentions. In the South, Egypt's foreign policy was to maintain the Jewish state of Judah as a buffer against Babylonian pressure. Not unlike the old cold war scenario where West Germany seemed to be the central front, Judah found herself in a very uncomfortable position. The prophetic question par excellence of the day was: how do these present realities concur with the promises of Yahweh? The whole covenant is centred on a promise to Israel that she will be secure in a promised land. What then do we make of this historical threat to our existence? Can we even conceive of the possibility of Babylonian captivity? And the prophets of the day split along the lines of whether such an event was conceivable and what it could mean.

Enter Jeremiah. Jeremiah is a prophet of the end of history. But unlike Fukuyama history does not end because it has come to its fulfilment or its completion. Rather, history ends when the symbolic world, or cultural myth, disintegrates. History ends when a community has no future and when all of the mythical sureties that have sustained it have collapsed. You see, on one level, Jeremiah and Fukuyama agree. Historical discernment must go beyond material considerations of shifting political, military and economic realities.

Communist Eastern Europe did not collapse just because the food lines were too long, or because wages were too low. No, the collapse of the regimes of Hungary, Poland, East Germany, Romania and Czechoslovakia is indeed, as Fukuyama argues, the collapse of a worldview, of an ideology. So also Jeremiah insists that the Babylonian military threat which will come from the North isn't just an unfortunate geo-political development in history that could perhaps be counteracted with a strategic alliance with Egypt. Rather, the military events on the horizon are a sign of a crisis of much greater proportions—a crisis in the symbol world and mythology of the royal and cultic establishment in Jerusalem.

Jeremiah's terrifying word is that Nebuchadnezzar's army to the north is nothing less than God's pending judgment on Judah. Indeed, Nebuchadnezzar was Yahweh's *servant*, ordained to bring judgment. As early as the first chapter of the book of Jeremiah, Yahweh says that he will use Babylon to come *against* Judah and that Jeremiah his prophet is called 'to uproot and tear down, to destroy and to overthrow, to build and to plant' (1:10). As Yahweh is against Judah, so also must Jeremiah be against Judah and against her kings, princes, priests and people (1:17-19).

At this point any similarity between Jeremiah and Fukuyama breaks down. You see, Fukuyama *works for* the kings and princes. He is a prophet of the royal court. If there is one thing that the royal court cannot countenance it is anyone telling it that its time is up, its days are over, it is not immortal. So what do the royal prophets, the State Department bureaucrats say when history is at its end? How do they interpret the ending of historical-cultural epochs, the decline of their own empires and the collapse of the mythic structures that have legitimated and guided those empires? They cover it up. They use mythical-cultural doubletalk to shield the king, the princes, the President, the Prime Minister—indeed, to shield themselves from the terrible realities that are before them.[29]

When history ends—whether it be the destruction of the Jewish covenantal world of monarchy and temple in 587, or the present dismantling of the Enlightenment dream of progress in an ever expanding consumer society—a culture experiences a terrifying sense of loss of control. Cultural disequilibrium sets in and history is experienced in terms of radical discontinuities. And if there is anything that imperial rulers (whether they be George Bush or King Jehoiakim) must maintain at all costs— even if the truth must be sacrificed and they have to put their heads into the sand—it is control, equilibrium and continuity. This is what these federally paid prophets will provide.

Commenting on Jeremiah's conflict with the royal priests and prophets, Walter Brueggemann says,

... Jeremiah's contemporaries are caught in an ideology of continuity and well-being in which human reality is covered over by slogans. The ideology sponsored by the crown and blessed by the temple is powerful, so that it carries all before it. Juxtaposed to such a powerful combination stands Jeremiah, armed only with a poem to act out his grief. The reality of grief is brought to speech against the slogans of success.[30]

Fukuyama is a prophet of such an ideology of continuity and well-being. He covers up human reality with his slogans of success. Bruce Cockburn has no use for such slogans:

Can you tell me how much bleeding
It takes to fill a word with meaning
And how much, how much death
It takes to give a slogan breath
And how much, how much, how much flame
Gives light to a name
For the hollow darkness
In which nations dress[31]

It doesn't matter whether the slogans are the Stalinist lies of a classless society or the Thatcherite lies of economic prosperity, they are both slogans and they are both lies. They both cover up the reality of pain and oppression. Such slogans are bought and sustained at a high price.

Endings have to do with death, the end of history, the end of life secure in the promised land, the end of Stalinist communism, the end of capitalism's growth mentality and world dominance. All such endings are times of grief. Something has died. It is funeral time. It is time for mourning, for weeping. Ultimately, it is time for repentance.

But grown adults, especially kings, prime ministers and presidents, don't cry. Self-secure bureaucrats don't cry. Instead, they congratulate themselves. The prophets of Jerusalem become prophets of continuity, security and the success of the present. Listen to Jeremiah:

'From the least to the greatest, all are greedy for gain;
prophets and priests alike, all practice deceit.
They dress the wound of my people

> as though it were not serious.
> "Peace, peace", they say, when there is no peace.
> Are they ashamed of their loathsome conduct?
> No they have no shame at all;
> they do not even know how to blush.
> Therefore they will fall among the fallen;
> they will be brought down when I punish them',
>   says the Lord (7:13-14).

Things will be OK. Peace, peace, the temple of the Lord, the temple of the Lord! (7:4) There is no threat. The structures of the myth (the constitution, democratic elections, the market system, the universities, the shopping malls) are all in place. Nothing will change. Don't worry! Go back to sleep!

That is what this kind of prophecy does—it puts you to sleep. I understand that Ceausescu, Honnecker and Jarazowski were masters at putting people to sleep until the people of Eastern Europe woke up to their reality. And now Fukuyama, George Bush, Brian Mulroney and John Major put us to sleep with false prophecies of peace that numb us to our socio-historical anxiety and pain.

These people are so numb, says Jeremiah, that they don't even have enough feeling left in them to blush. Feelings of shame are systematically denied and repressed, because if they allowed themselves to have such feelings they could no longer sustain their prophetic cover-up. As I suggested in the last chapter, historical denial results in numbness, in a lack of pathos—a-pathy—and in a lack of passion or compassion. Such prophets cannot tell the time. Fukuyama may suspect that it is the end of history, but he has no idea what time *that* is. He may be a little sad and bored. Perhaps he is nostalgic for the good old days of the Cold War when you knew the good guys from the bad, but he does not mourn, he has no grief.

Jeremiah, however, can't help himself. He is overwhelmed with grief. He has heard the word of the Lord. He has read the times correctly.

> Your wound is incurable
> your injury beyond healing.

> There is no one to plead your cause,
> no remedy for your sore,
> no healing for you (30:12-13).

And Jeremiah, the prophet of tears, knowing that,

> The harvest is past,
> the summer has ended,
> and we are not saved.

finds himself saying,

> Since my people are crushed,
> I am crushed.
> I mourn, and horror grips me (8:20-21).

> Oh that my head were a spring of water
> and my eyes a fountain of tears!
> I would weep day and night
> for the slain of my people (9:1).

Again, it is Cockburn who echoes Jeremiah for us today:

> You and me—we are the break in the broken wheel
> Bleeding wound that will not heal
> Lord, spit on our eyes so we can see
> How to wake up from this tragedy[32]

Cockburn and Jeremiah know what time it is. It is time to cry. It is time to grieve. It is time to mourn. And it is precisely because of this willingness to embrace the horror of the end of history—a willingness to grieve and weep and, indeed, to uproot, tear down, destroy and overthrow—that they can begin to rebuild and replant.

The biblical view of history, indeed the very structure of biblical faith, is one of radical reversals. Endings are never the final word. Historical endings always give birth to new beginnings. Funerals become festivals, death leads to resurrection. But—and this is an indispensable but—there are never new beginnings, festivals and resurrection without the prior reality of terrible endings, mournful funerals and violent deaths. Biblical faith knows 'that anguish is the door to historical existence, that embrace of ending permits new beginnings'.[33] The prophetic task is to cut through the numbed-out false security of those who, in their satiation, are closed to history, by giving public expression to pain and grief. This is, of course, the heart of the life and the teaching of Jesus of Nazareth, who said, 'Blessed are you who weep now, for you will laugh', and 'Woe to you who laugh now, for you will mourn and weep' (Lk 6:21,25).

Again, Walter Brueggemann sums it up well when he says, 'Only grief permits newness'.[34] Those who do not want the new are afraid of grief—they deny it to themselves and suppress it in others. But grief permits newness because grief, mourning and tears are not expressions of powerless acquiescence. No, it is the numbed-out sleepy old mumblers of 'peace, peace' who have acquiesced and are powerless because history is closed for them. Rather, grief, mourning and tears function as radical critique of the present order, because such mourning refuses to cover-up and insists that we confront the brokenness, oppression, failed expectations and empty promises of the present.

Such prophetic tears dismantle the present principalities and powers and make us impatient with their continued oppressive and deceitful rule. We become frustrated with history and ask, with Bruce Cockburn,

So how come history takes such a long, long time
When you're waiting for a miracle[35]

You see, prophetic grief is not just frustration with the present, it is also anticipation of the future. Grief not only *permits* newness, it is anticipatorily *rooted* in the hope of newness.

Fukuyama is sad because there is nothing new left for history. It seems to me that a Christian prophetic perspective is not only sad, but that it deeply mourns the present ending of history. Such a perspective lives, nonetheless, in the hope that this ending is not the final one and that there is a future of newness coming. This newness is not the product of our autonomous historical culture-forming, but a gift of the freedom of

God—a miracle we must wait for. We wait, however, not passively, but with tears and as co-partners in God's coming kingdom. And this is why we can sing with Bruce Cockburn that

> with pain the world paves us over
> Lord let us not betray
> God bless the children with visions of the Day.[36]

Notes

1 Cited by Jeremy Rifkin in *Time Wars: The Primary Conflict in Human History* (New York: Touchstone Books, 1987), p. 15.

2 *Ibid.*, p. 59. Rifkin refers to these temporal orientations as 'anthropological time zones'.

3 Cited by Rifkin, p. 62.

4 (New York: William and Morrow Co., 1986).

5 For a biblical reflection on who the history-makers are see Walter Brueggemann, *Hope Within History* (Atlanta: John Knox, 1987), ch. 3.

6 'Feast Of Fools' © 1978 Golden Mountain Music Corp. Words and music by Bruce Cockburn. Taken from the album *Further Adventures Of*. Used by permission.

7 'The Trouble With Normal' © 1983 Golden Mountain Music Corp. Words and music by Bruce Cockburn. Taken from the album *The Trouble With Normal*. Used by permission.

8 Francis Fukuyama, 'The End of History?', *The National Interest* (Summer, 1989), pp. 3-18. All page references in the text are to this article.

9 Allan Bloom, *The Closing of the American Mind: How Higher Education Has Failed Democracy and Impoverished the Souls of Today's Students* (New York: Simon and Schuster, 1987).

10 Whether Kojéve or Fukuyama are correct in their interpretation of Hegel is something that I will reserve judgment on. Though it should be said that one of the best Hegel scholars in the world today, Charles Taylor, insists that Fukuyama and Kojéve read Hegel's idealism as the simple inversion of Marx's materialism, and this misses the range and subtlety of Hegel's thought. See 'Balancing the Humours: Charles Taylor Talks to the Editors', *The Idler* 26 (Nov. and Dec., 1989), p. 21.

11 In this light the war against Iraq during the winter of 1991 is simply one of these skirmishes between a historical society that has not

yet noticed that the Absolute Idea has been actualised and the post-historical societies of the American-led coalition.

12 Though again, perhaps a war against one of those more primitive historical societies is just the thing to reintroduce a little excitement into our post-historical boredom.

13 *Ibid.*

14 Jack Cahill, 'Dark Victories: Capitalism KOs communism but not everyone is celebrating', *The Toronto Star* (Sunday 17th December 1989), B, pp. 1 and 4. See also Laurence Shames, 'What a long, strange (shopping) trip it's been: Looking back at the 1980's', *Utne Reader* 35 (Sept./Oct. 1989), pp. 66-71. It needs to be noted that this North American class analysis is based solely on economic factors, unlike the more complicated class structure in Britain.

15 Fukuyama declares that fascism is dead. I suspect that the obituary is premature. Cf. Robert Heilbroner's disturbing projections in *An Inquiry into the Human Prospect* (New York: W W Norton, 1974). For a literary portrayal of a similar fascist prospect see Margaret Atwood, *The Handmaid's Tale* (Boston: Houghton Mifflin, 1986). The existence of movements such as the National Front in Britain also makes my point.

16 Parenthetically I might add that the only difference between the two party system of the United States and the one party statism that has characterised the soviet bloc until very recently is 'one'. And that one extra party seems to make very little difference indeed in terms of addressing fundamental questions of political/ideological choice.

17 Cf. Jack Cahill, 'Dark Victories', *op. cit.*

18 'Call It Democracy' © 1985 Golden Mountain Music Corp. Words and music by Bruce Cockburn. Taken from the album *World Of Wonders*. Used by permission.

19 Heilbroner, *An Inquiry into the Human Prospect*, *op. cit.*, p. 83.

20 Cited by Rifkin, *Time Wars*, *op. cit.*, p. 165.

21 'Broken Wheel' © 1981 Golden Mountain Music Corp. Words and music by Bruce Cockburn. Taken from the album *Inner City Front*. Used by permission.

22 Peter Berger, *The Social Reality of Religion* (Harmondsworth: Penguin, 1973).

23 *Ibid.*, p. 27.

24 *Ibid.*, p. 32.

25 *Ibid.*, p. 95. Please excuse the non-inclusiveness of the language here. Berger wrote before the widespread rise of feminist consciousness. Incidentally, Fukuyama writes after the rise of such consciousness but does not appear to have noticed it.

26 Cf. Langdon Gilkey, *Reaping the Whirlwind: A Christian Interpretation of History* (New York: Seabury, 1976), pp. 47-69.

27 Rifkin, *Time Wars, op. cit.*, p. 154.

28 Gilkey, *Reaping the Whirlwind, op. cit.*, p. 54.

29 During skirmishes with peoples still mired in history they speak of 'collateral damage' when they mean that innocent civilians have been killed by bombs that were not as smart as they were supposed to be.

30 Walter Brueggemann, *The Hopeful Imagination: Prophetic Voices in Exile* (Philadelphia: Fortress Press, 1986), p. 43.

31 'Justice' © 1981 Golden Mountain Music Corp. Words and music by Bruce Cockburn. Taken from the album *Inner City Front*. Used by permission.

32 'Broken Wheel' © 1981 Golden Mountain Music Corp. Words and music by Bruce Cockburn. Taken from the album *Inner City Front*. Used by permission.

33 Walter Brueggemann, *The Prophetic Imagination* (Philadelphia: Fortress, 1978), p. 60.

34 Brueggemann, *Hopeful Imagination, op. cit.*, p. 41.

35 'Waiting For A Miracle' © 1987 Golden Mountain Music Corp. Words and music by Bruce Cockburn. Taken from the album *Waiting For A Miracle*. Used by permission.

36 'God Bless The Children' © 1973 Golden Mountain Music Corp. Words and music by Bruce Cockburn. Taken from the album *Night Vision*. Used by permission.

4

Waiting for a miracle: Christian hope at the end of history

Pilloried saints

I began this book by asking whether you would ever think to characterise the role of Christianity in the present world as being subversive. And as I have been investigating that question throughout the first three chapters I have had repeated occasion to draw upon the insights of two prophets, one very modern, the other very ancient. They are, of course, Bruce Cockburn and Jeremiah respectively. They are both subversive poets. This does not mean that I intend to canonise Cockburn, but it does mean that I sense a profound kinship between Cockburn and Jeremiah. They both address perilous times from a perspective that is rooted in the ways of God in history. They both proclaim the radical inversions of history that we have come to expect from prophets.

Toward the end of the last chapter I quoted the rather lamentful question in Cockburn's song, 'Waiting for a Miracle':

> So how come history takes such a long, long time
> When you're waiting for a miracle[1]

There is also a line in this song, however, that could be read to make a direct connection between Cockburn and Jeremiah. It is found in the first stanza of the song:

> Look at them working in the hot sun
> the pilloried saints and the fallen ones

working and waiting for the night to come
and waiting for a miracle

The phrase that makes me think of Jeremiah is 'pilloried saints'.
A pilloried saint is a saint who has been placed in the 'stocks',
that is, in a painful and humiliating device of incarceration.
Cockburn uses the metaphor to conjure up a picture of people
working under oppression. In the Bible there are only three
people who are said to have been placed in the stocks. There
are only three 'pilloried saints' in the Bible. They are Paul, Silas
and Jeremiah. Before looking at Jeremiah, let me briefly tell you
the story of Paul and Silas.

Paul and Silas had been preaching in Philippi with some
limited success when they encountered a young slave girl who
had a spirit in her that gave her powers to predict the future.
The girl followed Paul and Silas around day and night shouting,
'These men are servants of the most high God, who are telling
you the way to be saved' (Acts 16:17). Finally, almost in ex-
asperation, Paul commanded the spirit to leave the girl and she
was immediately liberated from its power. The problem is that
this act of exorcism had a negative economic impact on the
owners of the slave girl. It seems that they had been making a
comfortable profit on her fortune-telling abilities which were
now lost with the departure of the spirit. So they grabbed Paul
and Silas, brought them to the only appropriate place for an
economic crime to be tried, namely the marketplace, and ac-
cused them of stirring up trouble in the city and advocating
customs that are unlawful to all Romans. In other words, Paul
and Silas were subverting the Pax Romana. But more importantly they were engaging in a ministry that undercut certain
people's economic security. Consequently, they were stripped,
beaten, severely flogged, thrown into jail and placed in stocks.
Pilloried saints![2]

Jeremiah's experience with the stocks is similar, except that
Jeremiah was placed in the stocks not by Gentile Romans but by
his own fellow members of the covenant community. Jeremiah's crime? Proclaiming the end of history. Jeremiah's pro-

phetic word that the history of the royal/temple ideology in Jerusalem and Judah was coming to an abrupt and violent end at the hands of the Babylonians so angered the chief officer in the temple (a priest named Pashhur) that Pashhur had Jeremiah beaten and placed in the stocks (Jer 20:1-2). Pashhur represents the temple establishment. He would have been one of those who would have piously mouthed 'the temple of the Lord, the temple of the Lord, the temple of the Lord' (7:4) as an incantation to legitimate and secure that temple establishment. Jeremiah's prophecy flies in the face of this ideology. It declares that all such self-congratulatory language is nothing less than false prophecy. Consequently, Pashhur as custodian of the temple ideology deals with Jeremiah swiftly by means of a public flogging and being placed in stocks. Another pilloried saint. Another subversive who must be silenced. As usual, however, this pilloried saint is neither intimidated nor repentant. When released the next day he summarily changes Pashhur's name to Magor-Misabib, which means 'terror on every side', and repeats his prophecy of the impending judgment of Yahweh. Pashhur, agent of the temple which should be a place of shalom, is now given a name which foretells the terror that the end of history portends.

Jeremiah again

I have become convinced that the analogies between Jeremiah's time and our own are profound.[3] We share with Jeremiah a sense that historical life is precarious. Therefore, if we are to live with a sense of hope in the midst of this precariousness, and insist that that hope is not cheap, but deeply in touch with the pain, a-pathy, numbness and enculturation that we have been talking about in this book, then perhaps Jeremiah can offer us that kind of hope. Before looking at a specific (though rare) moment of hope in Jeremiah, however, I will first introduce you to this prophet in a way that is a little more complete than what was offered in the last chapter.[4]

Jeremiah becomes a 'pilloried saint' because, like Jesus who followed him, he proclaimed the shocking news of the prophetic inversions of history. Those who are blessed experience curse. Those who are to be the bearers of shalom embody terror. That which is secure is overthrown. Indeed, the very wording of Jeremiah's call sets him on a collision course with the leaders in Jerusalem. He is called 'to uproot and tear down, to destroy and overthrow' and only then 'to build and to plant' (1:10). Consequently he is told to 'stand against the whole land—against the kings of Judah, its officials, its priests and the people of the land' (1:18b). And it is precisely because he embodies this passionate ministry of judgment that his words and deeds of hope, of building and planting, have such power.

Jeremiah's conflict with the various kings of his day and their religious attendants in the temple centred around this question: is the Davidic covenant a covenant of inviolable rights? Is Yahweh's covenant with Israel such that the king can assume the security of his throne because the God who has been domesticated in the temple will always support him? The whole Jerusalem hierarchy assumed that this was to be the case. That is why they are the 'peace, peace' sayers. Jeremiah's response is unequivocal. Yahweh is *not* the patron saint of the king! Nor does he guarantee the king's security. In fact, Yahweh has become nothing less than the king's enemy.

This conflicting interpretation of the covenant had immediate implications for the question of how one discerns the times of history. Jeremiah's time is one of vast geo-political shifts and posturing. During his ministry he witnessed the fall of both Assyria and Ninevah and the marginalisation of Egypt. And, he 'watched the relentless and haughty rise of Babylon as *the* new power before whom all tremble'.[5] For the temple prophets it was impossible to even consider that the rise of Babylon could spell the end of Judah. Such a historical development would nullify the very religious foundation of Israelite society. Yet this is precisely what Jeremiah proclaims. The evil and cruel imperial power of Nebuchadnezzar's Babylon is the hand of God. Nebuchadnezzar is the servant of Yahweh. 'Unimaginable!', say the Jerusalem establishment. 'Treason!', shouts the royal court. This man is a subversive.

Jeremiah's subversion, however, is not simply a matter of a differing opinion concerning geo-political developments. Jeremiah would not make a very good guest on a television news show, simply proffering an alternative expert analysis. His subversion is much more profound. His is a proclamation that imagines the unimaginable. He subverts, through his imaginative poetic ministry, the dominant and domineering worldview that had kept his people numb to their own sin and their own pain.

This subversive prophecy shakes people out of their numbness in two ways. First, it discerns God's hand in history in such a way that impossible and unimaginable reversals take place. To get a sense of just how radical Jeremiah's proclamation was, imagine how you would have responded if, on 13th January 1991 (the Sunday before the war against Iraq began) the preacher at your church proclaimed: 'Thus says the Lord, "Because you have departed from my ways, have forgotten my faithfulness to you, have used your power and privilege to oppress and exploit, and have copulated with the god of economic growth, I have raised up my servant Saddam Hussein to punish you and take you as his slaves. And you, Presidents Bush and Mitterand, and Prime Ministers Major and Mulroney, will be taken from your opulent seats of power and languish the rest of your days in a Baghdad prison cell."' How would you have responded to something like that? Well, it certainly would be the case that agencies like the Royal Canadian Mounted Police, FBI and Scotland Yard would start taking some interest in your pastor. But you would likely have called the elders of the church together, perhaps got in touch with the denominational officials, and found some way to deal with your pastor who had clearly 'lost it'.

What we need to hear in Jeremiah is that his proclamation was just as 'off the wall' and radical as this, and more so! In the dominant worldview of that time not only was the king secure on his throne and God domesticated in his temple, but also, that royal/temple establishment was seen to be nothing less than the centre of the world. Within the mythic structure of the time, the

centre of the world was obviously where God dwelled. And
that was in the temple. And the temple was beside the royal
palace. And both were in Jerusalem. And beyond Jerusalem
was Judah. And beyond Judah was the rest of the world. And
all of these function as concentric circles with the temple in the
middle. It is the centre of the world. If Jeremiah had known
Yeats' line (from his poem 'The Second Coming'), I am sure he
would have quoted it: 'The centre cannot hold.' The centre of
the world is going to fall. And it will fall because God abandons
it.

Yahweh says, 'do you want to know what I think of the
temple of the Lord? Then look at what I did to Shiloh' (cf 7:14).
Shiloh was a shrine in the Northern kingdom of Israel that was
destroyed because of disobedience by the Philistines in 1050 BC.
Brueggemann comments that this historical memory of the
destruction of Shiloh

> ... was also a part of the rationale and self-understanding of
> the Southern royal community that Northern Shiloh and
> southern Jerusalem are precise opposites... Jeremiah vigor-
> ously denies this self-serving, ideological contrast and argues
> that Jerusalem is just like Shiloh. It is just like Shiloh in that it
> must obey to survive. It is just like Shiloh in its profound
> disobedience. And therefore, it is just like Shiloh in that it
> must be destroyed.[6]

Of course this is an impossible proclamation. It cannot be
believed. Perhaps another analogy would help to give us the
sense of the radical nature of this prophetic word. It is as if your
pastor preached a sermon after the war against Iraq was finished and said, 'You know how Baghdad was so severely destroyed in the winter of 1991? Well that is the way Washington,
London and Ottawa are going to look!' But perhaps we are too
numb, too comfortable even to consider such possibilities.

Jeremiah has another way to shake us from our enculturated
slumber, however. He wakes us up with loud, bitter, painful
and mournful weeping and wailing. He cries. This brings us
back to the theme of mourning from the last chapter. Jeremiah
is the weeping prophet not because he is emotionally insecure,

but because he is the prophet of the weeping God. Jeremiah knows that with the destruction of the temple, and with the departure of Yahweh from the temple something is lost. Something has died. And the only appropriate response is tears. The old sureties of Yahweh's faithfulness for ever and ever to this particular cultural reality are all gone. History, at least *this* history, has ended.

For Jeremiah that ending is inextricably connected to, or manifest in, an end to life in the land. History ends for the people of the promised land when that land is taken away from them and they are expelled from it in exile. This connection is inextricable not only because the identity of the covenant people is tied to their place in a land of promise (though that is important) but, more foundationally, the connection is inextricable because the covenant was never only with the people in the land, it was also with the land itself. All covenants are rooted in the covenantal relation that God has with all of creation. And when God's appointed image-bearers break covenant with Yahweh (as we saw in Chapter 1) the result is that the inheritance becomes 'detestable' (2:7).

> You have defiled the land with your prostitution and
>   wickedness.
> Therefore the showers have been withheld,
>   and no spring rains have fallen (3:2b-3a).

The irony here is biting. Precisely by screwing around with fertility gods and by seeking to manage and control the land through these gods, the opposite is the result—a defiled land and drought. No fertility.

Jeremiah's mourning, then, is not just for the sake of the people but also in solidarity with the land and with all of creation. Listen to his various laments for and with the land:

> I looked at the earth,
> and it was formless and empty;[7]
> and at the heavens, and their light was gone.
> I looked at the mountains,
> and they were quaking;

all the hills were swaying.
I looked, and there were no people;
every bird in the sky had flown away.
I looked, and the fruitful land was a desert;
all its towns lay in ruins
before the Lord, before his fierce anger.

This is what the Lord says:

'The whole land will be ruined,
though I will not destroy it completely.
Therefore the earth will mourn
and the heavens above grow dark,
because I have spoken and will not relent,
I have decided and will not turn back' (4:23-28).

How long will the land mourn
and the grass in every field be withered?
Because those who live in it are wicked,
the animals and birds have perished (12:4a).

The land is full of adulterers;
because of these things the land mourns
and the pastures in the desert are withered (23:10).

Judah mourns,
her cities languish;
they wail for the land,
and a cry goes up from Jerusalem.
The nobles send their servants for water;
they go to the cisterns
but find no water.
They return with their jars unfilled;
dismayed and despairing,
they cover their heads.
The ground is cracked
because there is no rain in the land;
the farmers are dismayed
and cover their heads.
Even the doe in the field
deserts her newborn fawn
because there is no grass.
Wild donkeys stand on the barren heights
and pant like jackals;

their eyesight fails
for lack of pasture (14:2-6).

O land, land, land,
hear the word of the Lord! (22:29)

Jeremiah presents us with a picture of total ecological break-down, nothing less than a de-creation. As we read his portrayal of the doe abandoning her fawn, the donkeys going blind from lack of pasture, and the disappearance of animals, birds and people, our hearts break. The creation that is called to respond to its creator in joy and song, mourns. Jeremiah mourns with the creation as we mourn the despoliation of creation in our time, in service of life-denying idols.

Jeremiah, however, was not surprised by this process of de-creation and consequent exile. As a prophet deeply rooted in the covenantal tradition of Israel he knew what happens when life in the land is taken out of its covenantal context and is presumed to be an eternal possession, not a gift of the Cre-ator-Redeemer. He knew that when the land is defiled through the service of false gods, the land itself reacts by vomiting out the idolatrous inhabitants.[8] Israel becomes the vomit of creation! As we have today.

If the covenant is inextricably connected to the land, and if Jeremiah's mourning is in solidarity with the land, then any hope that will be equal to this situation—any transformation that can turn this weeping into laughing (this cross into a resurrection)—must also entail a hope for the land. A heavenly hope that has no relation to life in this creation simply won't be good enough.[9] What we find in Jeremiah 32 is that the prophet surprisingly finds hope precisely in a small piece of land. To that story we now turn.

Real estate at the end of history

Picture this situation. You are in a war zone. The enemy has the city totally surrounded. You are in jail as an enemy sym-pathiser. Your charge? Treason! And then your cousin comes to see you in jail and offers to sell you a piece of family property.

The only problem is that that piece of property is now behind enemy lines. Does this sound like a very intelligent real estate transaction? Not likely. In fact it would be seen by any real estate agent as simply throwing your money away. Yet sometime during 588/587 BC this was precisely the situation that Jeremiah found himself in, and wouldn't you know it, he bought the land. The story is found in Jeremiah 32.

The picture that I have painted in this book of Western culture at the end of the twentieth-century is rather grim. Indeed, many people who share this perception of our present cultural crisis often find it very difficult to find any basis for hope that empowers them to go on. The numbness of those who say 'peace, peace' is often paralleled by the cynicism and paralysis of those who say 'woe, woe'. It is precisely to avoid that kind of cynicism and paralysis that I turn to Jeremiah 32.[10] If anyone had good cause for a paralysing despondency it was Jeremiah. He takes no joy in the fulfilment of his prophecies. Yahweh may well have chosen Nebuchadnezzar as his servant but Jeremiah could find no comfort in watching the Babylonian army take over the promised land. And now he was imprisoned as a pro-Babylonian traitor. Where can someone in such a situation find hope? In this story Jeremiah finds hope in what at first glance appears to be an insane real estate transaction.

Jeremiah's cousin Hanamel came to see him in prison with a deal that any shrewd business man would happily refuse. There is a field in Anathoth that is part of Jeremiah's family inheritance. Hanamel wants to sell it. And well he might want to sell it. Under the present circumstances it is economically worthless. It is behind enemy lines! There is no way that Hanamel can plant crops on it. And even if he did there is no guarantee that the Babylonian soldiers would give him a fair price on the produce (during a time of war they would probably have simply taken what they wanted). And there is also no guarantee that the Babylonians will continue to recognise Israelite traditions of familial ownership of the land either. So Hanamel wants out. But in Israel a landowner must first offer to sell his inheritance to a kinsman, a relative. This was a law that attempted to ensure that land was tied to family and not placed on a free market in which speculators could increase their holdings, thereby widening the gap between rich and poor.[11] In fact, the purchasing of family land was not so much a right in Israel as it was a high responsibility. Not exercising this familial responsibility during times of financial crisis was taken to be a very shameful thing. Hanamel makes explicit reference to this law when he says to Jeremiah, 'Buy my field at Anathoth in the territory of Benjamin. Since it is your right to redeem it and possess it, buy it for yourself' (32:8).[12]

Jeremiah immediately recognises this invitation to be nothing less than the word of the Lord and the text goes on in some detail to describe the transaction that followed, the amount of money involved, the witnesses and the deposition of the legal documents to seal the deal (vv. 9-14). Essentially, all that is going on here is a normal legal transaction between relatives within the context of the covenantal life of Israel. But it is precisely the normality of all of this that makes it so astounding. These were not, remember, normal times. Indeed, this is a normal (or normative!) transaction which is intended to maintain covenantal shalom in the land in the most abnormal of circumstances. It is an act of normativity, of covenantal law-keeping, in the context of societal anomie, a fulfilment of the law in a lawless situation, an ordering of a chaotic world. We have here a land transaction on the verge of total landlessness, on the verge of exile! And because this action is all of the above, it is also an act of *hope* in the face of *despair*.

Buying land under such conditions is an act of hope that flies in the face of all the empirical (indeed, imperial!) evidence. Yet, I suspect that the text goes on to give us the information about the transaction with some detail in order to highlight for us how normally legal and everyday all of this is. It seems to me that the text is saying that in the face of the end of history and of cultural collapse, the most radical thing that one can do is to continue to engage in normative shalom-bringing cultural activities. What should you do when the Babylonians are at the door? Buy some land behind enemy lines! And do it in front of witnesses (vv. 12-13) so that everyone will be able to see your hope.

In verse 15 it becomes clear why this transaction can occur in this seemingly impossible context. Jeremiah can buy this land because he has the vision to look beyond the present calamity, beyond the present ending, beyond grief, beyond land loss, defilement, Babylonian siege, drought and exile.

> For this is what the Lord Almighty, the God of Israel, says:
> Houses, fields and vineyards will again be bought in this land.

It is in the light of that hope and in anticipation of that restoration that Jeremiah can buy a field. This field is, as it were, a downpayment on that hope. We live our lives in terms of hope.[13] And if there is no possibility for renewal, return, reconciliation, if there is no hope for redemption (indeed, the redemption of land, of all of creation), then in the face of exile, of the end of history, despair is the only option. If that is the case then you might as well be numb. You might as well deaden yourself to your own hopelessness, because without hope we are paralysed in history. Jeremiah, however, breaks through this numbness and this paralysis with a radical act of hope. He buys the field.

In Jeremiah's prayer that follows this story (vv. 17-25), as well as in Yahweh's twofold response (vv. 26-35, 36-44), it is clear that such radical hope in history can have no foundation other than the redeeming action of God. It is, after all, the God who creates all things by his 'great power and outstretched arm', who by that same arm rescues Israel from slavery in Egypt and establishes her in a land flowing with milk and honey, that instructs Jeremiah to engage in the apparently absurd act of buying a field precisely when he is bringing judgment upon Israel by means of Babylonian seige (vv. 17, 21, 22, 24-25). But the meaning of that act of real estate investment can only be understood, says this text, against the backdrop not only of God's creative sovereignty, but also of his deep anguish and anger. This seems to be the point of the first part of Yahweh's response to Jeremiah's prayer.

It is intriguing that in the midst of a passage that is fundamentally about hope[14] the text returns one more time to the overwhelming theme of the book as a whole, namely judgment. It almost seems as if in verses 26 to 35 God is saying to Jeremiah, 'you are right, nothing is too hard for me' (in response to verse 17 of Jeremiah's prayer), 'including the destruction of Judah, the ending of her history, and the ending of her ideological pretensions'. But why tell us this again in the midst of the whole story about the field, in the midst of hope? Perhaps, this is God's way of saying, that yes we need hope, and that yes he is the only ultimate source of hope, but a definitive *no* to any kind of cheap hope: *no* to cheap grace. And in order to ensure that this grace is not cheapened, the text reminds us again of the context within which hope is offered. And that context is the abomination that the covenant people have become. Yahweh does not mince his words. 'The people of Israel and Judah have done *nothing but* evil in my sight since their youth; indeed, the people of Israel have done *nothing but* provoke me with what their hands have made, declares the Lord' (v. 30). Yahweh does not use very nuanced or balanced language here. 'Nothing but' evil, he says. Here we sense his profound anger. But at the end of this section he is not just angry, he is deeply perplexed.

> They built high places for Baal in the Valley of Ben Hinnom to sacrifice their sons and daughters to Molech, though I never commanded, nor did it enter my mind, that they should do such a detestable thing and so make Judah sin (v. 35).

Perhaps perplexity is not the word. Perhaps it is better to say that in his anguish, God is totally dumbfounded by what has happened. The reference is again to Molech. We met Molech earlier in Chapter 2 of this book when we compared our present generation's squandering of the creation to the sacrificing of children to Molech. At that point in the book we found the image most disturbing. In fact, when I first presented that material it was impossible for me to do so without tears in my eyes and a quivering voice. Here we find that God responds with a similar incredulity to such a thing. The act of child sacrifice is so abominable that God says that such a thing never even entered his mind. That is, not even God could have thought up something like this! It is almost as if he is saying such a thing even goes beyond the scope of his omniscience! 'I am totally blown away by this! I couldn't in my most depressed dreams have ever imagined that my people could do this.'

We have to hear the pathos in God's voice here. Because it is only if we can deeply hear this that we will be ready really to hear Yahweh's word of hope to us. It is only after immersing us again in God's anger and pain that the text then reflects more deeply on the meaning of hope found in the act of buying the field. This happens in verses 36 to 44. Go and buy a field, Jeremiah, because the Lord who brings the Babylonians to the door, who brings to an end the pretentious worldview of the West and Francis Fukuyama, and who brings judgment upon us for our idolatry is indeed the God for whom nothing is impossible. He is the God of hope! In stark contrast to what the people of Israel and Judah did in verses 30 to 35, this last section of this chapter is overwhelmingly about what Yahweh will do. Just note the action verbs:

> I will surely gather them ...
> I will bring them back ...
> I will give them singleness of heart ...
> I will make an everlasting covenant with them ...
> I will never stop doing good to them ...
> I will inspire them to fear me ...
> I will rejoice in doing them good ...
> I will give them all the prosperity that I have promised
>   them ...
> I will restore their fortunes ...

Prophetic reversals abound. Landless exiles will return to their inheritance. A fragmented community will experience single-ness of heart and unity. A broken covenant is replaced by a renewed covenant that is everlasting. The God who is sending them into exile promises to never stop doing good to them. In place of the terror of the Babylonians they will be inspired to fear the Lord. As God's anger and anguish is turned into rejoicing over doing good to them, so also is their weeping and mourning turned into laughing and dancing. And the creational blessing and wholeness that is the benefit of a covenantal relationship to God will once again be restored.

But what will be the evidence of all of this? The text is clear:

> Once more fields will be bought in this land of which you say, 'It is a desolate waste, without people or animals, for it has been handed over to the Babylonians.' Fields will be bought for silver, and deeds will be signed, sealed and witnessed in all the territory of Benjamin, in the villages around Jerusalem, in the towns of Judah and in the towns of the hill country, of the Western foothills and of the Negev because I will restore their fortunes, declares the Lord (vv. 43-44).

'That's it? That's what restoration is all about?' Precisely! 'But these are only the normal everyday kinds of things that we all experience in our lives in this world. Buying and selling fields, having legal witnesses, getting on with normal cultural life in the creation—*that* is what restoration is all about?' According to this text, and I believe, according to the biblical witness as a whole, this is precisely what redemption is all about—the restoration of creation and cultural activities in ways that please the Lord.

So then, what should we do to experience and bear witness to the hope that we have in Jesus Christ in such a time of crisis? We should go and buy some fields. In other words, the most radical thing that we can do as a Christian community at the end of history is to get on with our cultural life in all of its dimensions. Let me give you some examples. When the world system as a whole seems intent on sacrificing our children to the Molech-like god of economism, having children is a profound act of hope. The whole world seems to be falling apart around us. The future seems to promise little more than further economic collapse, geo-political confusion and an environmental nightmare. It takes faith and courage to bring children into this world with our eyes wide open.

Another example. In a marketplace that is characterised by cut-throat greed and near panic protectionism, Christian hope manifests itself in promoting and engaging in economic activities that promote a stewardly, environmentally sensitive and just sharing of creational resources for all people, but especially for the poor. Remember that the law that was obeyed in Jeremiah's buying of that field was a law designed specifically to ensure that there will be no poverty in the promised land. If we live with a hope that sees all of the creation as becoming the restored promised land then our economic activities must have the same focus.

The point is that one of the central ways in which we answer the question, 'how should we live?', is by answering the question, 'what are the contours of our hope?' If your hope is to be found in a heavenly life that is totally discontinuous with this earthly existence, then it is not surprising if the way in which that hope is manifest is simply in so-called spiritual exercises like fellowship, church-going, and personal evangelism. If, however, one has a hope in a new creation, a restoration of this creaturely life, then mundane things like buying fields behind enemy lines are powerful symbols of that hope. Buying such fields is a way of saying, 'even in the midst of all of this malaise, collapse and brokenness, this is still God's world and he will, indeed restore it'. What we need to do is to identify for ourselves what are the fields behind enemy lines that we need, in faith, to claim for our own. What are the fields of life that call for such redemption? What dimensions of our lives are presently oppressed by the captivity of powerful and destructive principalities and powers? I suspect that the answer to that question is literally, every dimension suffers under such oppression. Consequently, it is in every dimension of life that we need to engage in radical, and sometimes symbolic acts of a hope for life beyond captivity, beyond the present crisis. We need to find ways to experience God's shalom, God's redemptive presence, in all the dimensions of our lives, from the marketplace to the bedroom, from the board room to the classroom, from the theatre to the dining room.[15] In fact, there are many rooms to our lives, and it is in all of these rooms that we need to struggle together, in community, and with the healing presence of the Holy Spirit, to have a foretaste of a creationally restoring kingdom that is yet to come in all of its fullness.[16]

Still 'waiting for a miracle'

Of course, such a restoration is hardly imaginable to us. Indeed, it would be a miracle. But it is precisely for such a miracle that we actively await. This brings us back one more time to the images that Cockburn weaves together in his song, 'Waiting for a Miracle'. Look now at all of the lyrics of this song:

> Look at them working in the hot sun
> the pilloried saints and the fallen ones
> working and waiting for the night to come
> and waiting for a miracle
>
> Somewhere out there is a place that's cool
> where peace and balance are the rule
> working toward a future like some kind of mystic jewel
> and waiting for a miracle
>
> You rub your palm
> on the grimy pane
> in the hope that you can see
> You stand up proud
> you pretend you're strong
> in the hope that you can be
> like the ones who've cried
> like the ones who've died
> trying to set the angel in us free
> while they're waiting for a miracle
>
> Struggle for a dollar, scuffle for a dime
> step out from the past and try to hold the line
> so how come history takes such a long, long time
> When you're waiting for a miracle

This song was written in Managua in January of 1986, just seven years after the Nicaraguan revolution. And it gives expression to a tempered hope that resonates well with the hope of Jeremiah. It also gives voice to the kind of hope that I have been struggling to give voice to in this chapter. There is no militant triumphalism in this song. No sense that now that the dictator Somoza is gone Nicaragua will be a promised land of peace and abundance.[17] Rather this is a tempered hope—tempered by suffering and disappointment. Those who are waiting for a miracle are not just the 'pilloried saints', but also 'the fallen ones'. Hope is for those who know despair. In Cockburn's song it is those who are working out in the hot sun who know what it means to hope for the coolness of night. It is those who know the pain of oppression and war who can hope for a place where 'peace and balance are the rule'. Indeed, if you 'rub your palm on the grimy pane in the hope that you can see', you must have already known previously that in fact your vision was profoundly distorted and blurred. And it is only those who know that the past has led us down a dead end that will attempt to 'step out from the past and try to hold the line'. And it is only such people who can ask with integrity, 'so how come history takes such a long, long time, when you're waiting for a miracle?'

In Chapter 3 I suggested that Christian *grief* at the end of history is not a passive melancholy, but a passionate rejection and subversion of the way things are in the light of a profound vision of the way things ought to be. Such tears can be empowering. Now I want to take that thought one step further. Christian *hope* at the end of history is indeed a *waiting* for a miracle. The kingdom of God, the restoration of creation, is not something that we produce. Hence, triumphalism will only result in disappointment and cynicism. But neither is such a waiting passive. Indeed, precisely because we wait for a miracle are we empowered to be 'working toward a future like some kind of mystic jewel'. This is an active waiting. The action of the 'pilloried saint' named Jeremiah was to buy a field behind enemy lines. Cockburn's 'pilloried saints' are out working that field 'in the hot sun'. Both are giving expression in the midst of ordinary day to day culture-forming tasks of a profound hope. That is the hope of a subversive Christianity.

Notes

1   'Waiting For A Miracle' © 1987 Golden Mountain Music Corp. Words and music by Bruce Cockburn. Taken from the album *Waiting For A Miracle*. Used by permission.

2   I won't take time to tell the rest of the story here about the earthquake and Paul's insistence in the end that he be treated with the dignity of a Roman citizen, but encourage my readers to go and spend some time with this wonderful story in Acts 16.

3   My understanding and appreciation for Jeremiah was deeply enhanced through co-teaching a course with J Richard Middleton at the Institute for Christian Studies in Toronto that spent the majority of its exegetical efforts in this book of the Bible. Again my debt to Richard is acknowledged.

4   There are innumerable secondary sources on this prophet, all of which shed some light on who he was and on the character of his ministry. The author who best captures Jeremiah's passion, however, is Walter Brueggemann. Cf. his *Jeremiah 1-25: To Pluck Up, To Tear Down*, International Theological Commentary Series (Grand Rapids and Edinburgh: Eerdmans and The Handsel Press, 1988); 'The Book of Jeremiah: Portrait of the Prophet', *Interpretation* 37 (No 2) (April, 1983), pp. 130-45; and 'Prophetic Ministry: A Sustainable Alternative Community', *Horizons in Biblical Theology: An International Dialogue* 11 (No 1) (June, 1989), pp. 1-33. For Brueggemann's critical evaluation of some of the major commentaries on Jeremiah that have been published in the 80s, see his essay, 'Jeremiah: Intense Criticism/Thin Interpretation', *Interpretation* 42 (No 3) (July, 1988), pp. 268-80.

5   Brueggemann, 'The Book of Jeremiah', *op. cit.*, p. 138.

6   Brueggemann, *Jeremiah 1-25*, *op. cit.*, p. 77.

7   Jeremiah here portrays the land in a state of de-creation. The phrase 'formless and empty' is *tohu wabohu* and remembers back to the state before the forming and filling of creation in Gen 1:2.

8   Cf. Lev 18:24-25, 28; 20:22.

9   The creation-affirming and renewing nature of redemption is addressed at further length in my co-authored book, *The Transforming Vision* (Downers Grove: IVP, 1984), pt 2. See also Al Wolters, *Creation Regained* (Grand Rapids: Eerdmans, 1985), and Steve Shaw, *No Splits* (London: Marshall Pickering, 1989).

10 Since the following paragraphs attempt to exegete certain dimensions of this text the reader is encouraged to have Jeremiah 32 open in front of her as she reads.

11 This was the ancient law found in Leviticus 25:25-31. It is parallel to the Levirate law of Deuteronomy 25:5-10, which was appealed to in the story of Ruth.

12 It is interesting to note that as cousin Jeremiah is not Hanamel's closest kinsman. The implication of this is that Hanamel must have approached other relatives with no success before coming to Jeremiah. The other relatives were not prepared to exercise their familial and covenantal responsibilities under such circumstances.

13 Bob Goudzwaard calls this our 'horizon of happiness'. *Capitalism and Progress*, translated by Josina Van Nuis Zylstra (Toronto and Grand Rapids, Wedge and Eerdmans, 1979), p. 139ff.

14 Jeremiah 32 occupies a place in what has come to be called the 'Book of Consolation' in the text of Jeremiah as a whole. This 'book' encompasses chapters 30 to 33.

15 This book does not attempt to be a 'how-to' book and therefore I will refrain from being more specific here. I avoid such specificity for three reasons. First, there are numerous other books on an alternative lifestyle available that I can heartily recommend that deal with these issues better than I could. (I refer you especially to books like D J Longacre, *Living More With Less* (Scottdale, PA: Herald Press, 1980) and Steve Shaw, *No Splits* (London: Marshall Pickering, 1989); for books that deal with the wide range of academic disciplines from a Christian perspective see 'A Bibliography We Can't Live Without', compiled by Brian Walsh and Richard Middleton, in James Sire, *Discipleship of the Mind* (Downers Grove: IVP, 1990), pp. 219-243.) Secondly, the purpose of this book is to help you form your worldview. As such I am more concerned with the matter of setting free our imaginations. Thirdly, I firmly believe that the 'how-to' of such a lifestyle is better formed in the day to day life of a Christian community than by the pontifications of an outside author.

16 I am indebted to my friend and colleague James Olthius for this metaphor of the rooms of our lives.

17 Such triumphalism could be detected, however, in some of Cockburn's earlier songs about the Nicaraguan revolution. I am thinking of 'Nicaragua' and 'Dust and Diesel' from his 1984 album *Stealing Fire*.

Postscript

Subversive Christianity 22 Years Later

What Time Was It?
What time is it?

IN MANY RESPECTS, THIS was the overriding question of *Subversive Christianity*. More than twenty years ago I wrote this little book with the subtitle, *Imaging God in a Dangerous Time. What time is it?* I asked. It was a dangerous time. A time of cultural captivity for the church in the midst of what I discerned to be a time of cultural collapse.

The dominant metaphor in the book was Babylon. We live, I suggested, in Babylon and the church runs the fatal risk of being captivated by a Babylonian imagination, rooted in Babylonian narratives, symbols, practices and worldview.[1] So in chapter one I argued that it is time for the church to be set free from Babylon by embracing anew the liberating narrative of the scriptures, specifically Israel's creation story and its view of humanity created in the image of God.[2] And in chapter two I argued that it is time for

---

1. Shortly after the publication of this book, N.T. Wright and I developed a model of understanding worldviews in terms of narrative, ultimate questions and answers, symbols and praxis. The model first appeared in Wright's *The New Testament and the People of God* (Minneapolis: Fortress Press, 1992) and was further developed in my co-authored book with Steven Bouma-Prediger, *Beyond Homelessness: Christian Faith in a Culture of Displacement* (Grand Rapids, Eerdmans, 2008), ch. 4.

2. The exegesis of Genesis 1 and 2 was indebted to the work of J. Richard Middleton. Middleton and I developed this vision of the imago dei in contrast to Babylonian (and modernist/postmodern) notions of humanity in *Truth*

the church to abandon its safe dualisms and intellectualism and to open its eyes to a new discernment of the times. *What time is it?* It is time for the people of God to see that we are at the end of an idolatrous cultural experiment and to be awakened to a new imagination of life in the Kingdom of God.[3]

When telling time in the early 1990's, however, I could not ignore the massive geo-political shifts that were afoot with the collapse of the Soviet Union. And if I were to analyze the world-historical significance of that collapse, I had to also engage the seminal thesis of Francis Fukuyama's essay, "The End of History?" Fukuyama had a way of telling the time that proclaimed the unabashed victory of economic and political liberalism. He argued that there was no longer any viable alternative to a democratic capitalist ideology and that we would see the ineluctable spread of consumer society, not just because Western political and economic forces have proven inescapable, but more significantly because such an economic and political liberalism is nothing less than the 'end of history.' This was where history has always been going. This was the *telos* of history. Employing a Hegelian perspective, Fukuyama perceived the triumph of liberalism over communism wasn't a contingent event in history, but the self-actualization of the Absolute Idea itself.

The influence and popularity of Fukuyama's essay, not least in Christian intellectual circles, demanded a response. So, concluding that Fukuyama was a false prophet, in chapter three I introduced him (at least in the pages of this book) to two other prophets: contemporary singer-songwriter, Bruce Cockburn, and that ancient disturber of the peace, Jeremiah. Fukuyama was a little

---

is Stranger than It Used to Be: Biblical Faith in a Postmodern Age (Downers Grove, Ill.: InterVarsity Press, 1995), ch. 6. Middleton's subsequent book, *The Liberating Image: The Imago Dei in Genesis 1* (Grand Rapids, Brazos Press, 2005) has become the standard work on this subject. My debt to Richard has only deepened over the years.

3. This critique of intellectualism, together with an emphasis on imagination has been articulated more recently by James K. A. Smith in his two books, *Desiring the Kingdom: Worship, Worldview and Cultural Formation* (Baker, 2009) and *Imagining the Kingdom: How Worship Works* (Baker, 2013).

melancholic about the end of history, and maybe a little bored. Cockburn and Jeremiah, however, weep and rage. Fukuyama kind of shrugged as he gave the West a congratulatory pat on the back for being in tune with the unfolding of Consciousness, being at the end point of history. Cockburn and Jeremiah greet the end of history with grief and lament.

And so I sat in that grief and lament throughout most of 1990. Of course I knew that this book could not end with my attack on Fukuyama. The book could not end with 'grief at the end of history.' But that was as far as I could go. Personally, I was devoid of hope . . . until I revisited both Cockburn and Jeremiah. Listening one afternoon to Cockburn's "Waiting for a Miracle" I heard, as if for the first time, the rest of the song. In chapter three I had only referred to one poignant and evocative line from that song: "So how come history takes such a long, long time/when you're waiting for a miracle?" But on that afternoon I heard anew the hope that pervades the song: the call not just to passively *wait* for a miracle, but to actively *work* in that waiting.

Then I returned to Jeremiah. There isn't much hope in Jeremiah—just four chapters out of fifty-two— but the hope that is to be found is audacious and radical while at the same time so everyday and mundane. Live a normal, indeed a covenantally normative, life in the midst of the empire. Redeem land behind enemy lines. Tell the exiles in Babylon to settle down, plant gardens, give and take in marriage and seek the shalom of the city, even if it is the city at the heart of the empire. *What time is it?* Time to engage in everyday lives of faithfulness, everyday lives of redemptive culture-making, and--against the odds, against the evidence--we find ourselves *working* and *waiting* for a miracle. Then the covenantal God promises that the miracle of homecoming, the miracle of restored life in creation, the miracle of the Kingdom of God will be ours.

What Time Is It?

Twenty years later and I am struck by how revelant the message of this book remains. The sense of both cultural captivity and collapse has, if anything, intensified over the years. And if events such as the fall of the Berlin Wall and the stock market crash of 1987 ("Black Monday") were important historical markers for discerning the times in the early 90's, then undoubtedly the fall of the twin towers in 2001 and the stock market crash of 2008 are similar, and perhaps even more poignant, markers for telling time in the second decade of the twenty-first century.[4]

So let's revisit our three conversation partners twenty years later. What would Fukuyama, Cockburn and Jeremiah have to say to us about our socio-economic and geo-political reality today?

Fukuyama Revisited

The temptation for a Postscript like this would be to offer a detailed analysis of everything that Fukuyama has written since he became an intellectual celebrity of the neoconservative movement twenty years ago. That would be a worthwhile project but this is not the place for its realization. We can, however, ask how Fukuyama has responded to the two most formative historical events of the last two decades: 9/11 and the crash of 2008.

It would seem reasonable to conclude that the ascendancy of George W. Bush to the White House, with his administration's entrenchment in a neoconservative geo-political and economic ideology, would only serve to prove Fukuyama's thesis of the end of history. When President Bush told the nation on the evening of 9/11 that the forces of chaos had attacked the heart of civilization, one could hear echoes of Fukuyama's distinction between historical and post-historical societies. These groups on the margins of progress, still mired in history with its ideological debates, have launched an attack on the very nation in which history has come

---

4. My failure to discuss the significance of the 1989 Chinese student protests in Tiananmen Square continues to be a weakness of this book.

to its fulfillment, its end. And when the President ended his four minute speech to the American people, and the rest of the world, with the words "America is still open for business," one might well have thought back to Fukuyama's observation of the ineluctable spread of consumerist culture. If the 'end of history' is that humans are homo economicus, that we are 'born to shop,' that well-being is defined in terms of economic affluence, then the boldest thing that the President could say to America's enemies, and the most comforting thing that he could say to a nation in shock would indeed be "America is still open for business."[5]

It all sounds like Fukuyama's perspective has won the day. But let's stop to ask: How does Francis Fukuyama discern the times in post 9/11 America? Not with another self-congratulatory pat on the back, but with some serious reconsideration. Fukuyama's 2006 book *America at the Crossroads: Democracy, Power, and the Neoconservative Legacy* reads as an attempt to not only distance himself from the Bush administration, but also to argue that he is not to blame for the folly of that administration. While never quite recanting his previous argument in the "The End of History?" he does conclude that "neoconservatism, as both a political symbol and a body of thought, has evolved into something that I can no longer support."[6] Again, this is not the place to trace out his analysis of the evolution of this body of thought, or his role in that evolution, but it is important to see how Fukuyama tells the time at this juncture in history, this 'crossroads' for America.[7]

---

5. Sylvia Keesmaat and I reflected on this speech in our book, *Colossians Remixed: Subverting the Empire* (Downers Grove, Ill.: InterVarsity Press, 2004), 35-37.

6. Francis Fukuyama, *America at the Crossroads: Democracy, Power, and the Neoconservative Legacy* (New Haven and London: Yale University Press, 2006), xxxi.

7. I appreciate the argument that we should refuse to use the term "America" to refer to the United States because there are many nations in the "Americas". Perhaps as a Canadian this hasn't mattered that much to me because Canadians don't really identify as "American" in any continental sense. For this discussion, however, I will follow Fukuyama's more limited use of the term as a synonym for the United States and its citizens.

Fukuyama notes that prior to the election of George W. Bush, neoconservative intellectuals "proposed a foreign policy agenda involving concepts like regime change, benevolent hegemony, unipolarity, preemption and American exceptionalism."[8] These ideas became the hallmark of the Bush administration, and Fukuyama finds all of them to be fundamentally mistaken.

He observes that the kind of regime change that we saw in Iraq has been a dismal failure, making the country a hotbed for the most extreme forms of Islamic jihadism.[9] But more troubling for Fukuyama is that the Bush administration's notion of regime change amounted to nothing less than an exercise in social engineering in a foreign nation and culture, without regard to the organic socio-religious and historical conditions of that country. Attempting to socially engineer Iraq into a democratic liberal state amounts to little more than a revived Leninism of the right as opposed to the left. "I did not like the original Leninism," writes Fukuyama, "and was skeptical when the Bush administration turned Leninist. Democracy in my view is likely to expand universally *in the long run*."[10] It cannot be artificially imposed or engineered.

But what about the neoconservative conviction that in a unipolar world where the United States is the only superpower left standing, America has a responsibility to exercise a benevolent international hegemony? Or to put this question in terms that

8. Ibid., 3.

9. In this 2006 book, Fukuyama wrote this concerning Iraq: "The scale of the problem has grown because we have unleashed a maelstrom; whatever the merits of the original intervention, walking away from Iraq now without creating a strong and stable government there will leave a festering terrorist sanctuary in the Sunni triangle." (p. 185) The events in Iraq in the late Spring and early Summer of 2014 have proven him right.

10. Ibid., 55. Indeed, later in the book he writes, "There is simply no other legitimating set of ideas beside liberal democracy that is broadly accepted in the world today." (p. 130) Note that this is a decidedly softer position than the Hegelian determinism that we saw in "The End of History?", but not totally out of line with that original thesis. If liberal democracy is the natural unfolding and actualization of the Absolute Idea, then there is no need to force the matter by regime change. Eventually, in one way or another, we will all find ourselves embraced in this post-historical moment.

perhaps Fukuyama would find less palatable, what about the business of a benevolent American empire? Hasn't the unfolding of history placed this burden of empire upon America, and isn't it precisely this historical unfolding that demonstrates and proves the doctrine of American exceptionalism that has been embedded in its mythology from its inception? Fukuyama quotes the neoconservative writers William Kristol and Robert Kagan, who argue that in foreign policy the United States "does not pursue a narrow, selfish definition of its national interest but generally finds its interests in a benevolent international order." They go on, "In other words, it is precisely *because American foreign policy is infused with a high degree of morality* that other nations find they have less to fear from its otherwise daunting power."[11] Fukuyama wryly comments, "It is hard to read these lines unironically in the wake of the global reaction to the Iraq war."[12] Indeed, he acknowledges with some understatement that "benevolent hegemony rests on a belief in American exceptionalism that most non-Americans simply find not credible."[13]

Without a doctrine of benevolent hegemony rooted in American exceptionalism, every dimension of the Bush administration's response to the attacks of September 11, 2001 is proven to be fundamentally mistaken, especially the doctrine that legitimates America and America alone to engage in preemptive attacks on other states or perceived terrorist threats within those states. Add to this the clear deceitfulness of the administration's justification for the invasion of Iraq because somehow Iraq was connected to 9/11 and Sadam Hussein had 'weapons of mass destruction' when the administration knew that both of these claims were lies (and there was nothing 'noble' about them), and it is not surprising that Francis Fukuyama wants to abandon the term 'neoconservative.'[14]

---

11. Cited by Fukuyama, Ibid., 102 (emphasis added by Fukuyama) from William Kristol and Robert Kagan, *Present Dangers: Crisis and Opportunity in American Foreign and Defense Policy* (San Francisco: Encounter, 2000), 22.

12. Ibid., 102-103.

13. Ibid., 111.

14. Indeed, it almost seemed as if the Bush administration successfully

America is at a crossroads, Fukuyama argues. America needs to abandon notions of regime change, benevolent hegemony and maybe even exceptionalism, and embrace a foreign policy more concerned with development, international institutions, and the employment of soft power rather than the blunt hard power of military intervention. All of this means "a dramatic demilitarization of American foreign policy and reemphasis on other types of policy instruments."[15] Fukuyama knows that no one outside of the United States believes in benevolent hegemony or American exceptionalism. No one outside of the United States believes in the moral superiority of the American political system, economy or people. And insofar as we have found ourselves in a unipolar world, that very unipolarity has resulted in a marked rise of anti-American sentiment around the world.

Perhaps Fukuyama is here abandoning the self-congratulatory arrogance of "The End of History?" and embracing a kinder, gentler and more humble notion of historical unfolding. The disaster of the Bush administration's foreign policy, the dismal failure of its military adventurism, its patent deceitfulness, and the precipitous decline of America's international reputation all require a radical rethinking of this time in history.

What happened on 9/11 was one thing. What happened during the week of October 10, 2008, however, was something altogether different. The "Armageddon" of Monday, October 19, 1987 was echoed in the "Nightmare on Wall Street," "Banking's Black Monday," a "Day of Reckoning," and the beginning of "The Week that Broke Wall Street" of Monday, October 6, 2008. That day the Dow Jones Index dropped 800 points and continued to drop for the rest of the week. The crisis spread around the world, impacting all national economies, but especially those most vulnerable to fluctuations in the financial markets. Financial institutions went

---

engaged in mass hypnosis of the American people. Just repeat "9/11 and Iraq" over and over again in the same sentence and before long people will simply assume that the two things are connected. This is the classic deceitfulness of empire.

15. Ibid, 184.

bankrupt, and even more were bailed out by worried national treasuries, most notably the Federal Reserve in the United States. By the end of the week the head of the International Monetary Fund warned that the world financial system was "on the brink of systemic meltdown."

We need to be clear that what came crashing down in 2008, and what had to be bolstered up by the tax payers, wasn't the economy of production and consumption of real goods. Rather, what crashed in 2008 was the financial markets: that shady world of currency speculation, subprime mortgages, and various kinds of derivatives where money chases money in order to produce more money. In fact, 98% of all economic transactions every day in the world have to do only with the financial markets. This is a virtual economy, not a real economy.[16] This is capital circulating the world "driven by its quest for maximum short term financial gain . . . ."[17]

What got so bloated that it burst in the fall of 2008 was the financial market which essentially trades in money. Remember the language that was used to describe this collapse: we were in a financial "bubble" and the bubble burst.[18] The Christian economist Bob Goudzwaard, however, speaks more evocatively of a "bloated financial sector."[19] Bloated, full of foul smelling gas that needs to

16. In an essay with Nancy Birdsall, Fukuyama also acknowledges the distinction between the financial sector and the 'real economy.' They write, "Free capital markets can indeed allocate capital efficiently. But large interconnected financial institutions can also take risks that impose huge negative externalities on the rest of the economy in a way that large manufacturing firms cannot." "The Post-Washington Consensus: Development After the Crisis," *Foreign Affairs* 90.2 (Mar/April 2011), p. 47. They go on to say that "open capital markets combined with unregulated financial sectors is a disaster in the waiting." The crisis of 2008 was manufactured precisely by the high stakes gambling of the financial markets.

17. Bob Goudzwaard, "Globalization, Economics, and the Modern Worldview," in Michael W. Goheen and Erin G. Glanville, eds., *The Gospel and Globalization* (Vancouver: Regent College Publishing/Geneva Society, 2009), 114.

18. John Ralston Saul, *The Collapse of Globalism* (Toronto: Penguin, 2009), 291.

19. Bob Goudzwaard, Mark Vander Vennen, David Van Heemst, *Hope in Troubled Times: A New Vision for Confronting Global Crises* (Grand Rapids, MI: Baker, 2007), 142.

be released. Bloated with an obscene wealth that can only rot and grow putrid within the economic systems of the West. Bloated because it grew beyond any natural bounds. "We have put our trust in the financial markets to save our real economies. But now the idol is staggering . . . and we can make out more clearly its profound betrayal."[20] This kind of economy creates a high degree of turbulence and volatility. We had been playing with fire and had an explosion in 2008 that all the government bail outs in the world could not extinguish.[21]

While Francis Fukuyama has not used the language of idolatry to describe the economic collapse in 2008, he does use the language of 'sacrifice' in a recent article, evocatively titled, "The Future of History: Can Liberal Democracy Survive the Decline of the Middle Class?"[22] Curiously enough, for someone who once said we reached end of history because the debate of ideology had finally been settled, in this essay Fukuyama calls for nothing less than the production (his metaphor) of a new ideology to see us into the future. And this ideology "would begin with a critique of the elites that allowed the benefit of the many to be *sacrificed* to that of the few and a critique of the money politics, especially in Washington, that overwhelmingly benefits the wealthy."[23]

Fukuyama observes:

> There is a broad correlation among economic growth, social change, and the hegemony of liberal democratic ideology in the world today. And *at the moment*[italics mine], no plausible rival ideology looms. But some very troubling economic and social trends, if they continue, will both threaten

20. Bob Goudzwaard, "A Note about the Credit Crunch, Climate Change and Environmental Responsibility," accessed on line at http://empiremixed. com/2008/10/08/a-note-about-the-credit-crunch-climate-change-and-environmental-responsibility/#more-222.

21. Goudzwaard, et. al., *Hope in Troubled Times,* 141.

22. *Foreign Affairs* 91.1 (January/February, 2012).

23. Ibid., p. 61. Emphasis added.

the stability of contemporary liberal democracies and dethrone democratic ideology as it is now understood.[24]

"At the moment" there are no rivals to liberal democratic ideology, but this ideology can be both threatened and dethroned. Gone is the Hegelian bravado of the early 1990's, to be replaced with a much more humble and tentative position.

Following others, I argued that the erosion of the middle class in western liberal democracies both indicated the triumph of capitalism and contained the seeds of its own demise. Fukuyama is now making the same observation. In this essay he notes that median incomes in the United States have stagnated since the 1970's, while there has been a growth in massive inequality in incomes: "In 1974, the top one percent of families took home nine percent of GDP; by 2007, that share had increased to 23.5 percent."[25] And there has been no leveling out of this inequality post 2008. We have not only seen the decline of the middle class, we have entered into a new Gilded Age of massive inequality in the midst of the richest nations on earth.[26]

So what do we need to do? Fukuyama's proposals would seem to amount to a total abandonment of his earlier position. We need to construct a new ideology that will "reassert the supremacy of democratic politics over economics and legitimate anew government as an expression of the public interest . . . The new ideology would not see markets as an end in themselves; instead, it would value global trade and investment to the extent that they contributed to a flourishing middle class, not just to greater aggregate national wealth."[27]

At the heart of it all, the narrative that was celebrated in the 1990's as the inevitable victor and necessary outworking of

24. Ibid., p. 58. Emphasis added.

25. Ibid.

26. This is carefully documented in Thomas Piketty's celebrated book, *Capital in the 21st Century* (Cambridge, Mass.: Harvard University Press, 2014).

27. Ibid., p. 60

historical progress is now recognized as the failed ideology that it is. Fukuyama concludes his essay with these words: "The alternative narrative is out there, waiting to be born."[28]

Once you start talking about narratives waiting to be born, you have abandoned the narrowly scientific pretense of neoconservative ideology. Human life is rooted in narratives that are the foundation of all human imagination. But such narratives are particular and often in conflict with other ways of telling the story of our world.

So now, let's revisit another one of our dialogue partners, one who has spent his life telling stories of the world as he has experienced it, thereby weaving an alternative imagination. How would Bruce Cockburn tell the time, some twenty years after our first explorations of his music in this book?[29]

Cockburn Revisited

Unlike Fukuyama, Bruce Cockburn did not need to engage in any radical rethinking of his worldview in order to respond to the events of 9/11 or the crash of 2008. It is also not surprising that the one who sang it is "time for the silent criers to be held in love"[30] would respond to the unfolding of history since the fall of the Berlin wall with considerably more passion than does Mr. Fukuyama.

That passion is nowhere more palpable than on his post 9/11 album, *You've Never Seen Everything*. In his grief filled song, "All our Dark Tomorrows," George Bush is nothing less than the "village idiot" who "takes the throne." In a world characterized by Bush's "War on Terror," Cockburn sings,

28. Ibid.

29. I have addressed the contribution of Bruce Cockburn to a Christian imagination at greater length in my book, *Kicking at the Darkness: Bruce Cockburn and the Christian Imagination* (Grand Rapids, Brazos: 2011).

30. "Feast of Fools," from the album *Further Adventures of* (True North Records, 1978).

There's a parasite feeding on
Everybody's bag of rage
What goes out returns again
To smite the mouth and burn the page
Under the rain of all our dark tomorrows

I can see in the dark it's where I used to live
I see excess and the gaping need
Follow the money—see where it leads
It's to shrunken men stuffed up with greed
They meet and make plans in strange half-lit
   tableaux[31]

Bloodshed begets bloodshed, violence begets violence, and there is nothing redemptive to come from the Bush administration's response to 9/11.

On his next album, *Life Short Call Now*, Cockburn accuses President Bush of "projecting your shit at the world/self-hatred tarted up as payback time," and calls Mr. Bush to:

Tell the universe what you've done
Out in the desert with your smoking gun
Looks like you've been having too much fun
Tell the universe what you've done

Tell the universe what you took
While the heavens trembled and the mountains
   shook
All those lives not worth a second look
Tell the universe what you took[32]

---

31. "All our Dark Tomorrows," from the album *You've Never Seen Everything* (True North Records, 2003).

32. "Tell the Universe," from the album *Life Short Call Now* (True North Records, 2006). Cockburn continues to reflect on the Iraq war in his song, "This is Baghdad" on the same album.

So much for benevolent hegemony and American exceptionalism!

Yes, it is time for a new narrative to be born, but it must be a narrative that can tell the stories of the failures at the 'end of history.' It must be a story of unafraid honesty, that can see in the dark and tell, with tears flowing in deep sadness and lament, the stories of our ideological violence. We must still express 'grief at the end of history.'

Cockburn directly addresses the neoconservatism that Fukuyama has now abandoned in his song, "Slow Down Fast."[33]

> L ron N ron every kind of ron con
> Neocon old con got to put the brakes on
> Slow down fast

The neoconservative agenda was a con from the beginning. The dream of economic affluence was a numbing sedative to keep us asleep to the realities all around us.

> Oil wars water wars tv propaganda whores
> Fire alarm met with snores no one gets what's
>   gone before
> Slow down fast

The world is rushing towards economic and ecological oblivion and we're all caught napping. Cockburn wants to awaken us from our ideologically imposed slumber. Again, it is only in the language of abrasive and painful lament that we can break through the imagination of the empire that holds us captive.

While Fukuyama's "End of History" was oblivious to the ecological cost of consumer culture, and his more recent essay "The Future of History" also fails to reflect on the environmental crisis, Cockburn sees ecological destruction at the heart of our socio-historical crisis. Reflecting on species extinction, the artist sings,

---

33. "Slow Down Fast," from the album *Life Short Call Now*.

There's a knot in my gut
As I gaze out today
On the planes of the city
All polychrome grey
When the skin is peeled off it
What is there to say?
The beautiful creatures are going away[34]

Can an alternative narrative emerge without telling this story? Can any narrative be credible if it does not address "the callous and vicious things/humans display"? Can we find a way forward if we do not find a way to address the fact that as humans we seem invariably to "create what destroys" and "bind ourselves to betray"?[35]

And if we are to emerge on the other side of the financial collapse of 2008 and find a way to imagine our economic lives beyond the neoclassical capitalist ideology that got us into this mess, then won't we need to tell the unabashed truth about trickle down economics? Cockburn takes on this challenge in his jazz-infused song "Trickle Down:"[36]

Trickle down give /em the business
Trickle down supposed to give us the goods
Cups held out to catch a bit of the bounty
Trickle down everywhere trickle down blood

You see, the "captains of industry" are "smiling beneficently," but they are riding on a "leaking hole supertanker ship of fools." In this world of financial markets disconnected from the real economy of goods and real services, it's all . . .

Take over takedown big bucks shakedown
Schoolyard pusher offer anything-for-profit
First got to privatize then you get to piratize
Hooked on avarice - how do we get off it?

34. "Beautiful Creatures," from the album *Life Short Call Now*.
35. Ibid.
36. "Trickle Down," from the album *You've Never Seen Everything*.

There's the issue: we're hooked on avarice, addicted. And the condition is terminal: "Greed twists eternal in the human heart."[37] We have lost all sense of grace, of the common good, of care, as our imaginations are captivated by an ideology that can only bring curse, no room for blessing. The end of history indeed.

While Cockburn is still 'waiting for a miracle,' his patience in this waiting diminishes as he ages. I can relate. In "Wait No More," the artist has an apocalyptic sense of the crisis of our times ("wild things are prowling – storm winds are howling tonight"), together with a glimpse of redemption ("everything's transforming into pure crystals of light"). He yearns that "one day we'll wake to remember how lovely we are," but until then, he sings with an aching longing: "I don't want to wait no more."[38]

Curiously enough, another prophet of passion and lament counseled patience to those who wait.

Jeremiah Revisited

It is no overstatement to describe the presidency of George W. Bush as imperial in character. You don't have to be a left wing ideologue to observe that the Pax Americana of the Bush years, the centralization of coercive power legitimated in post 9/11 America, and the American exceptionalism that laced the rhetoric of the White House was all the stock in trade of empire.

How else might we understand a war in Iraq justified by fear and deceit? How else might we interpret the unilateralism of an administration disdainful of the United Nations, who withdrew from almost every important international treaty during its time in office? How else might we understand an ideological commitment to a neoconservative economic agenda that allowed the market to come to the verge of collapse in a morass of greed and corruption? And how else might we interpret a commitment to an American

37. "You've Never Seen Everything," from the album *You've Never Seen Everything.*

38. "Wait No More," from the album *You've Never Seen Everything.*

vision of prosperity and affluence that has willingly sacrificed the planet and the next generations on the altar of global capitalism?

Thank God that George W. Bush left the Oval Office on January 20 at 12.01PM. I've got the tee-shirt. But what about Barack Obama? Has his administration addressed the question of American empire?[39] That's the kind of question that Jeremiah might have wanted to ask. Has Obama redirected the American imagination from imperial rule to global service, from the arrogance of empire to the humility of stewardship, from an ideology of affluence to a vision of justice?

If most of us mark time by events like 9/11 and the Crash of 2008, then undoubtedly we also mark recent history by the remarkable election of the first African American president of the United States on November 4, 2008. What time is it now as we come to the end of the second term of Obama's presidency?

"Yes we can." Those three words captured the imagination of a nation. "Yes we can" awakened a hope that promised to bring America and the world out of the nightmare of the Bush administration into the dawning of a new day, a reawakening of what Obama loves to call "the American promise."

Those three words, "Yes we can" are rooted in three other words that are at the very foundation of the American experiment, "We, the people." And as I watched the tears flowing down Jesse Jackson's face on election night in 2008, I remembered Martin Luther King Jr. calling America to fulfill her promise, a promise so terribly cut short and belied by slavery and racism. And as a friendly neighbour to the north watching "the people" vote in record numbers in that election, I found that I wanted to believe Obama's "Yes we can." I wanted to believe that "We, the people" is a truly revolutionary sentiment, a radically liberating foundation for a nation.

I wanted to believe.

39. Within two weeks of Obama's 2008 election, Chris Hedges argued that those "clustered around Obama . . . have no interest in dismantling the structure of the imperial presidency and the vast national security state." History has proven him right. *The World as it Is: Dispatches on the Myth of Human Progress* (New York: Nation Books, 2013), p. 266.

I remain deeply uneasy, however, with the language about the American dream that pervades Obama's rhetoric. For example, when he proclaimed in his speech at the Democratic convention, "I will restore our moral standing so that America is once more the last, best hope for all who are called to the cause of freedom, who long for lives of peace, and who yearn for a better future," perhaps some people in the world were wondering, 'what moral standing?', 'what freedom?', 'what peace?', indeed, 'what hope for whose future?'

The problem is that a nation rooted in slavery and genocide, a nation with a bloody history of undermining and overthrowing governments unfriendly to American political and economic interests, a nation that has the largest military complex in the world, a nation that has had empire written all over it from its inception doesn't seem to be a nation with much of a moral standing. And to arrogantly claim that this nation, with this history, is the world's "last, best hope" would seem to be little more than an idolatrous and ideological nationalism that is unbecoming to anyone who would desire to follow Jesus and submit his political aspirations to the shape of the Kingdom of God.

Okay, perhaps that was a little over the top. Surely we can't dismiss America, nor Obama with his "New Dream for America" so quickly. And when he said at that convention, "America, we are better than these last eight years," I wanted to believe him. But what is at stake here is a discernment of the times, and a discernment of the American project.

Has the Obama presidency done more than broken with the imperial spirit of the Bush/Reagan dynasty, but also pulled away from the imperial historical imagination of America herself? Can you be a President of the United States of America and not be imperial?

How would Jeremiah discern the time in the midst of the Obama administration? Here's what's interesting and disturbing about this prophet. He begins his prophetic ministry in the context of the rule of King Josiah. Josiah, grandson of Manasseh who "shed much innocent blood" (2 Kings 21:16) and son of Amon who served the idols of his violent father, becomes king at age eight. And in his early 20's Josiah became the leader of an amazing reform movement in Judah. When the priest Hilkiah found the Torah in the Temple (that's right, it was lost and forgotten!) he gave it to Josiah and the king called for national repentance and began to clean house. Idolatry was outlawed, the places of idol worship were destroyed, the Passover was kept and the covenant was renewed.

I think that Josiah could have said something like, "Judah, we are better than we have been for the last number of years. We are a better people than this. We have a better promise than this. We have a deeper hope than this. By renewing covenant I will restore our moral standing so that the heirs of Abraham will once more be the last, best hope for all who are called to the cause of freedom, who long for lives of shalom, and who yearn for a better future." And he would have been right.

It is not surprising, then, that the writers of 2 Kings pronounce a favourable judgement on Josiah. "He did what was right in the sight of the Lord" (2 Kings 22:2). And Josiah is one of the very few kings about whom this is said.

But if Jeremiah shares this approval, he doesn't say. For some reason, Jeremiah never makes reference to Josiah's reforms. Jeremiah doesn't offer his political endorsement of this king who sought to renew the deepest hopes and most profound promises of Israel. In fact, at one point the prophet says,

> Run to and fro through the streets of Jerusalem,
> look around and take note!
> Search its squares and see if you can find one person
> who acts justly
> and seeks truth—
> so that I may pardon Jerusalem. (5:1)

Give me one guy who acts justly and seeks truth, and then the fall of Jerusalem might be averted! One guy!

And for some reason, Jeremiah doesn't reply,

"Well, there is King Josiah, after all. I mean Josiah's doing his best here. He's reaching into the richest memories of Israel, the deepest roots of her covenantal promises. Surely here is the one who acts justly and seeks truth."

But Jeremiah doesn't appeal to Josiah. We don't know why, really, but maybe Jeremiah felt that Josiah was too little, too late.

Indeed, the preface to the book of Jeremiah seems to say that the dye is cast. In the opening three verses we are told that these are the words of Jeremiah, to whom the word of the Lord came, from the 13th year of the reign of Josiah (that is, five years before the Josian reforms began) through the quick successive reigns of his sons, Jehoiakim and Zedekiah "until the captivity of Jerusalem." Note the terse telling of history here: from the 13th year of Josiah's reign until the Babylonian captivity. It reads as if the reforms had no impact on this trajectory of history. And even when, in the one other reference to Josiah in the book of Jeremiah (22:15–16), he is described as a king who did justice and righteousness by judging rightly the cause of the poor and the needy, this is only offered in contrast with the economic injustice, exploitation and opulence of his son, Jehoiakim. Perhaps Josiah was an honourable man, but his sons demonstrated that the practices of covenantal infidelity ran deep in the royal family of Judah.

Maybe Jeremiah felt that Josiah's reforms were not going to be radical enough to re-shape the very character of this idolatrous nation. Or maybe he felt that as well-intentioned and eloquently articulated as these reforms were, they didn't get to the depths of the rot and corruption of the national character.

For from the least to the greatest of them,
everyone is greedy for unjust gain . . .
They have treated the wound of my people carelessly,
saying, "Peace, peace,"
when there is no peace. (6:13,14)

They say, "we are a better country than this" but the prophet doubts it.

They reach into the best history they've got and speak glowingly of the "promise," but the prophet says, "Do not trust in these deceptive words: 'This is the temple of the Lord, the temple of the Lord, the temple of the Lord.'" This is the American Dream, the American Dream, the American Dream. Yes we can, yes we can, yes we can.

No, this prophet, writing during Josiah's reign says things like:

They went after worthless things and became worthless. (1:5)
You defiled my land. (1:7)
You have polluted the land with your whoring and wickedness. (3:2)
They take over the goods of others . . . they catch human beings . . . their houses are full of treachery . . . they have grown fat and sleek . . . they do not judge with justice. (5:26–28)
Truth has perished: it is cut off from their lips. (7:28)

Good thing that Jeremiah wasn't running for office.

When, during his first inaugural address, President Obama said that America was ready to "lead once more" and that he "will not apologize for our way of life," I wonder what Jeremiah would have thought. And while he might have appreciated his statement that the issue wasn't the size of the GDP "but the reach of our prosperity," Jeremiah might have pointed out that American prosperity had consistently been bought at the expense of both freedom and prosperity for much of the world. Or when Mr. Obama said to America's enemies that they would suffer defeat and yet "we will extend the hand if you unclench your fist," I wonder if Jeremiah might have been appalled at the lack of understanding of these enemies. Fists get clenched for a reason and they will seldom open because the threat is uttered with greater intensity. Bruce Cockburn might respond that "everything is bullshit but the open hand"[40] and that a clenched fist can only be transformed

---

40. "Strange Waters," from the album *Charity of Night* (True North

into an open hand when the initial reasons for that clenching are redemptively addressed.

President Obama spoke of hope over fear and unity over conflict. But can hope be found without repentance? Can such unity be achieved apart from apology? To the poorest of the poor, for those on the underside of the growing gap between rich and poor both in America and around the world, there is much for which to apologize. And surely someone needs to apologize for the murderous deception of the previous administration.

I don't know why Jeremiah never endorsed the reforms of Josiah. Surely Jeremiah's critique of Judah was rooted in the very Torah that Josiah had brought back into the national consciousness. And yet he refused to get on the reform bandwagon of this good king.

Might it be that all of Josiah's improvements notwithstanding, this Torah reform movement did not go far enough to radically transform Judah's historical imagination? Might it be that as good as Josiah was, he couldn't really countenance the thought that Judah was facing the end of its history? The end of the monarchy, of any notion of covenantal exceptionality, of any royal aspirations to benevolent hegemony, of the collapse of the temple, the very centre of the cosmos? Might it be that the centre did not hold and that all the Torah zeal in the world could not and would not bring it back together again?

The inviolability of the Davidic monarchy in the imagination of Josiah has its parallel in Barack Obama's foundational belief that America remains the world's "best hope" for freedom because of the exceptional nature of this nation and its people in history. Did we dare hope that President Obama could preside over the dismantling of the American empire? My hunch is that Jeremiah knew that Josiah could never have really imagined something like Babylonian exile. And if we stand in the tradition of Jeremiah, we should know that Obama could not possibly have an historical, geo-political vision that could imagine the radical decline of America.

Records, 1995).

Pulitzer prize winning journalist Chris Hedges, however, can imagine such a decline:

> The American empire, along with our wanton self-indulgence and gluttonous consumption, has come to an end. We are undergoing a period of profound economic, political, and military decline. We can continue to dance to the tunes of self-delusion, circling the fire as we chant ridiculous mantras about our greatness, virtue and power, or we can face the painful reality that has engulfed us. We cannot reverse this decline. It will happen no matter what we do. But we can, if we break free from our self-delusion, dismantle our crumbling empire and the national security state with a minimum of damage to ourselves and others.[41]

Hedges sounds like Jeremiah, until the last sentence. Hedges is more optimistic than his ancient counterpart. While Jeremiah called Judah to abandon the self-delusion of covenantal security, he had no illusions that anyone would be able to dismantle the crumbling kingdom of Jehoiakim and Zedekiah. Things were about to get ugly.

The end of history remains a time of grief. If we take our cue from Jeremiah and discern that we are in the midst of ecological, economic, socio-cultural and geo-political collapse then any tone of apocalyptic self-righteousness profoundly misses the point. The church is called to mourn and only out of our lament might hope be born. Only in a context of lament will we find a path of faithfulness in the midst of collapse. And only in lament will the church be released from her cultural captivity.

To return to Bruce Cockburn's rich imagery, we are working and waiting for a miracle. Waiting in grief and working in hope. We find ourselves, I think, somewhere at the interface of Psalm 139 and Jeremiah 29. The interface of sorrow at the end of history

41. *The World as It Is*, p. 277.

and hope through everyday covenantal life in the midst of empire. What do you do in Babylon? Sit and weep, sings the psalmist.

What do you do in Babylon? Build houses, plant gardens, eat good meals, get married and have children, writes the prophet.

The psalmist sings this blues song with a pathos that is palpable.

> By the rivers of Babylon—
> there we sat down and there we wept
> when we remembered Zion.
> On the willows there
> we hung up our harps.
> For there our tormentors asked for mirth, saying,
> "Sing us one of the songs of Zion!" (Ps. 137:1-3)

How about a little Israelite folk tune? How about a little cultural diversity here? How about a little entertainment?

> How could we sing the Lord's song
> in a foreign land?
>
> If I forget you, O Jerusalem,
> let my right hand whither!
> Let my tongue cling to the roof of my mouth,
> if I do not remember you,
> if I do not set Jerusalem
> above my highest joy. (Ps. 137:4-6)

These are songs of remembering, but reducing them to entertainment and singing them as a cover up of deep grief amounts to devastating forgetfulness. The psalmist will sing, but he will not sing the songs of that happy, sentimental and emotionally manipulative 'worship set' at the beginning of the service. No, the only song that can be on his lips in captivity will be the hard edge, bent and broken dissonance of the blues. Indeed, should he succumb to the temptation of cheap liturgy with its too-quick songs of lovely

Zion, should he practice this aesthetics of forgetting, then may the right hand that picks the tune on his harp whither and the tongue with which he sings such songs cling to the roof of his mouth, rendering him silent.

No, this psalmist won't cover it all up with pious sounds and language. He won't hide his disappointment, pain and anger. Rather, he will allow his full rage to be expressed and call for nothing less than pay back on his tormentors, than death to their children. "Happy shall they be who take your little ones and dash them against the rock!" (Ps. 137:9) Sometimes you have to say venomous words in order to get the violent rage out of your system.

That is one pole of living in empire. That is one dimension of facing the end of history with a brutal honesty. That is one way of confronting the violent collapse of your way of life and the degeneration of your deepest dream into your worst nightmare. That is one means of waiting for a miracle when history takes such a long, long time.

Such emotional rawness would have been no stranger to Jeremiah. And yet he will offer another path of response. Acknowledging that history will take a long time and that the time of captivity will not be short, he writes a letter to those in exile.

> Thus says the Lord of hosts, the God of Israel, to all
> the exiles whom I have sent into exile from Jerusa-
> lem to Babylon. (Jer. 29:4)

While not denying the ruthlessness or the historical agency of the Babylonians in this crisis, Jeremiah begins by saying that this exile is ultimately God's work, not the king of Babylon's.

> Build houses and live in them; plant gardens and
> eat what they produce. Take wives and have sons
> and daughters; take wives for your sons, and give
> your daughters in marriage, that they may bear
> sons and daughters; multiply there and do not de-
> crease. (Jer. 29:5-6)

The prophet who was called to "pluck up and to pull down, to destroy and to overthrow," is now finally able to fulfill his call "to build and to plant" (Jer. 1:10).

What do you do in exile, in imperial captivity? Get on with everyday, normal life. But how can we do that in a foreign land? How are we to get on with normal life in such an abnormal situation? How on earth could we have the heart and energy to build houses and plant gardens when we can't muster up the strength to pick up our harps and sing a couple of the old hymns?

Jeremiah's advice to the exiles begins to sound like a counsel of passivity and quietude. But that would miss the political realism, biblical depth and missional responsibility of his words. Jeremiah refuses to give easy answers that will evade the devastating reality Judah faces at the end of her history. Exile is for real. The collapse of all that was held to be secure and eternal must be understood for what it is, and there will be no quick resolution, no cheap optimism. Exile is for the long haul and the exilic community must find ways to live their lives in the midst of imperial captivity. This is Jeremiah's political realism and the church needs such open-eyed realism today.

This is a realism, however, rooted in a deep and liberating biblical memory. As soon as we hear a Hebrew prophet telling people in exile to "multiply and not decrease," we hear an allusion to Israel in Egypt. Subject to cruel brick quotas and violent overlords, the people of Israel "were fruitful and prolific; they multiplied and grew exceedingly strong" (Ex. 1:7). Such multiplication was the precursor to their liberation.

Moreover, whenever you meet the language of being fruitful and multiplying you hear echoes of the deepest of Israel's memory of creation. In that primordial blessing and calling of Genesis we hear the words, "Be fruitful and multiply, and fill the earth and subdue it" (Gen. 1:28).

I began this book with the argument that Genesis offers us nothing less than a story of human origins, calling and dignity that is subversive of Babylonian mythology and definitions. The vision of humanity, created in the image of God and called to a life of loving stewardship in creation, flies in the face of Babylonian notions of humans as the slaves of the gods, subject to the imperial rulers who represent those gods. So when Jeremiah echoes Genesis in his letter to the exiles, it is clear that this is no easy accommodation to Babylon. Rather, Jeremiah is calling the exiles to live out their creational and covenantal calling even in Babylon. Babylon does not define reality for you. Babylonian stories do not shape your imagination. Be fruitful and multiply. Practice your legitimate rule in creation, engage in culture forming as you were always called to do, subject not to the demeaning and ultimately deadly worldview of Babylon, but subject to your calling by the God of Israel, the God of all creation. Live out of these memories and Babylon will not be able to determine your future. Multiplying isn't just a matter of procreation; it's language geared to keep your imagination free from Babylonian captivity.

"Build houses and live in them," instructs the prophet. In the devastation of exile, create homes. When all has collapsed in an orgy of death, build and live. In the midst of a culture of wide-spread socio-economic, ecological and cultural homelessness, we are called to be radical homemakers.[42] Move into the neighbour-hood, create places of hospitality and refuge, advocate for the homeless, put down roots and engender a love and affection for this place because even Babylon can be a site of homemaking.[43]

"Plant gardens and eat what they produce," Jeremiah goes on. You may live in Babylon, but you need not depend on the Babylonian food economy. This may be exile, but the invitation to creational gardening remains at the heart of our identity as image-bearers of the Creator. Jeremiah calls the exiles to break free from the imperial control of food production and consumption. Indeed, in the movement toward community gardening and an

42. Shannon Hayes, *Radical Homemakers: Reclaiming Domesticity from a Consumer Culture* (Richmondville: Left to Write Press, 2010).

43. These themes are developed at some length by Bouma-Prediger and I in *Beyond Homelessness*. For the implications of this vision of shalom for urban ministry see Mark R. Gornik's powerful book, *To Live in Peace: Biblical Faith and the Changing Inner City* (Grand Rapids, MI.: Eerdmans, 2002).

agricultural model centred on place and care we can see some of the most creative and hopeful responses to life in empire.[44]

At the heart of it all, Jeremiah offers this vision of renewed, faithful, day-by-day cultural fruitfulness not as a survivalist manifesto, but as a call to shalom. His vision is politically realistic, biblically rich and missionally directed. "Seek the shalom of the city where I have sent you into exile, and pray to the Lord on its behalf, for in its shalom you will find your shalom" (Jer. 29.7). Israel is called to be a blessing and a light to the nations, including Babylon. Work towards shalom, the prophet says. As impossible as it might seem in the midst of such a violent and bloodthirsty empire, as counter-intuitive as it sounds in a world of exploitation and oppression, give your lives to the shalom of the empire. Here is a call to the common good, to a flourishing economy of justice and a regenerative ecology that is desperately needed in a globalized system that is collapsing all around us. Here is a vision of well-being and restored relationships that can animate a widespread movement of peace in a world perpetually at war.

Build houses in a culture of homelessness. Plant gardens in polluted and contested soil. Get married in a culture of sexual consumerism. Make commitments in a world where we want to always keep our options open. Multiply in a world of debt. Have children at the end of history. Seek shalom in a violent world of geo-political conflict and economic disparity. This is Jeremiah's word to the exiles. This is Jeremiah's subversive word to us. And in this vision we just might see, with Jeremiah, "a future with hope" (Jer. 29:11). This is what it means to work and wait for a miracle. This remains at the heart of a subversive Christianity.[45]

44. Keesamat and I discuss the question of what all of this looks like in our daily lives at some length and specificity in *Colossians Remixed*, especially in chapters 9 and 10.

45. My deep gratitude to Melissa Kuipers for her fine editing on this Postscript.